THE NEW ICE AGE

A Year in the Life of the NHL

STEPHEN BRUNT

THE NEW ICE AGE

A Year in the Life of the NHL

M&S

Canadian Cataloguing in Publication Data

Brunt, Stephen
The new ice age

Based on the CBC television series: The new ice age.
ISBN 0-7710-1711-1

1. National Hockey League.   I. Title.
II. Title: New ice age (Television program).

GV847.N3B78   1999   796.962'64   C99-930175-6

Book design by Ingrid Paulson
Typeset in Goudy by M&S, Toronto
Printed and bound in Canada

We acknowledge the financial support of the Government of Canada
through the Book Publishing Industry Development Program for
our publishing activities. We further acknowledge the support of
the Canada Council for the Arts and the Ontario Arts Council
for our publishing program.

McClelland & Stewart Inc.
The Canadian Publishers
481 University Avenue
Toronto, Ontario
M5G 2E9

1 2 3 4 5   03 02 01 00 99

AUTHOR'S NOTE

This book is based on the CBC Television series *The New Ice Age*, and contains dialogue (occasionally cleansed of robust hockey language) taken from footage shot by the producers. Each chapter mirrors the themes of one of the series' six episodes.

It is, however, a separate entity. The ordering and the arrangement of the material, along with the ideas and opinions expressed, are my own. The text is based both on the series and on experience and knowledge gained while covering the National Hockey League for the *Globe and Mail*.

Those ideas and opinions are not necessarily shared by the producers, White Pine Productions, or by the Canadian Broadcasting Corporation.

Stephen Brunt

CONTENTS

· MAKING IT ·

IT HAS BEEN FONDLED and kissed and filled with beer. It has served as a cradle for babies, a vase for flowers, an ornament on a bar, a passenger in trains, planes, automobiles and boats. It has been carried into strip bars, it has been left behind after drunken binges, it was once drop-kicked into the Rideau Canal. It is venerated like a religious relic, and it is used like a party favour. It is an ungainly hunk of silverware, the bowl a replica of the humble mug Lord Stanley bought for $50 and donated to the hockey champions of the Dominion in 1893, the collar a place to commemorate every person who can lay claim to it, 1,600 names in all. During the Stanley Cup finals, crowds have lined up all night just for a moment in its presence, in New York where it was so long coming, in Denver where it arrived all but instantaneously, in Canada, anywhere, where the Shroud of Turin wouldn't draw a bigger or more devout gathering. Children are held aloft to gaze at it and told to remember what they're seeing. Those at the other end of life's spectrum strain failing eyes for a glimpse to hold in memory. For any hockey fan, to see it sparkling from a distance is to imagine what it must be like to touch it, to hold it, to bear it aloft around the ice as the crowd stands and roars, to see your name inscribed among so many others.

Forget the comparisons. There is nothing else like it in all of sport. The Stanley Cup, to Canadians and others who have fallen under the spell of hockey, is more than just a trophy. It has come to symbolize the pure, perfect mesh of culture and sport. It's not just a prize, but an icon. For a player, to touch it is to touch the entire history of the game, to put your hand where Howie Morenz put his, to feel what Gordie Howe felt, or Rocket Richard, or Wayne Gretzky, to be connected to every childhood fantasy, every dream dreamed at dawn on the way to the local rink.

It says something about the game, about the passion of the athletes who play it, and about their innocence, their lack of cynicism, that the members of the winning team are still given the opportunity to take the Cup home. Just try to imagine that in baseball, in basketball, in football. Whereas the championship trophies in other sports are locked safely away before and after the presentation, the Stanley Cup goes on the road. Anyone who deals with professional athletes will tell you that none have a stronger bond with their sport than hockey players. None seem more grateful just to have the chance to be part of it. None retain so much of the joy of childhood, of play. What could be more fulfilling, then, than to take the Cup back to the place whence you came, back to family and friends and the people who watched you learn the sport. Each member of the winning team takes a turn doing just that.

The trophy is delivered to each member of the winning team in turn by its handlers from the Hockey Hall of Fame. It is removed from the special casket in which it travels. After that, it's up to the player where it goes. In the summer of 1997, members of the Detroit Red Wings took it on a long, wild ride, to points in Canada, in the United States and, for the first time, to Russia, where curious onlookers were at first perplexed and then dazzled. Whatever the place, the faces look the same when the Cup comes into view: joy, awe, wonder, seeing in the glittering a reflection of ourselves.

Joey Kocur of the Red Wings took the Stanley Cup fishing as part of the trophy's wild ride after Detroit's 1996–97 victory.

OF COURSE all of that happened in what most outsiders would consider the off season. And indeed, at the moment Steve Yzerman held the Cup aloft at Joe Louis Arena, presenting it to loyal fans of the Red Wings for the first time since 1955, one cycle came to a close, the long road to a championship with which every hockey fan is familiar. It starts just as northern climes are beginning to feel the first cold breath of winter. It ends, these days, in full-blown summertime, when it's a challenge even in the game's most northern outpost, Edmonton, to keep the ice from getting soft. In between, during the long winter months in the place where hockey roots run deepest, it is still the game that matters.

But there is another cycle as well – the cycle of hockey commerce. The National Hockey League is an entertainment business, growing ever bigger, more sophisticated, more international. The bottom line, as it has always been, is filling the seats in the arenas, selling tickets for a two- or three-hour diversion in a world where leisure-time options seem to multiply by the minute. It is also about selling T-shirts and jerseys and hot dogs and beer. It is selling private boxes and club seats to businesses and the wealthiest fans. It is selling programming to television networks, and by extension selling the products that will be advertised on those broadcasts. It is about selling new franchises in unlikely places, expanding the marketplace, increasing the options. It is moving beyond North America, and selling the *idea* of the NHL, of the world's fastest game, of the very best players in the very best showcase, around the world. Gary Bettman, the league's commissioner, has overseen the transformation of the business of hockey, the addition of powerful, enormously rich new owners, the acquisition of a U.S. network television contract, and the first real labour war in the game's history – the lockout of 1994–95.

In a sense, hockey is becoming what Canadians always hoped it would be – big time, big league, with the rest of the world finally understanding what they always understood was the best sport going. But that couldn't come without a cost, without changing the game in ways that weren't necessarily in the interest of the hockey heartland. As they say, be careful of what you wish for. It might come true.

There is a tension between those two elements, between Canadian fans and the head office on Park Avenue, between those who want to cling to hockey the way it is and the way it was, and those who must chart a path to an ever more competitive future. Sometimes, those interests are necessarily at odds.

Never was that more evident than in the hockey year that spanned parts of 1997 and 1998, one of the most tumultuous periods in the history of the game. During that time, the National Hockey League embarked on one of the most ambitious ventures in its history, shutting down the regular season for two weeks so that its players could participate in the Winter Olympic Games in Nagano. To set the stage for that tournament, some of the first games of the season were played in Tokyo. Expansion pushed ahead, with four new cities set to join the league by century's end – all of them in the United States. Player salaries reached all-time highs. Meanwhile, Canadian clubs, burdened by the tumbling dollar and by small-market economics, struggled to survive. The Edmonton Oilers would actually be on their way to Houston, Texas, before being saved by a group of local investors. Near season's end, a House of Commons committee was convened to examine the state of hockey – and other professional sports – in the country. Soon after they were out of the playoffs, it was revealed that the Ottawa Senators were verging on insolvency, unable to service their considerable debts.

At times, it felt like the culture of Canadian hockey, so evident in those Stanley Cup visits, so evident in the national depression that followed the Olympic tournament, had simply become incompatible with the commercial vision of the modern NHL and that the league's interests were no longer our interests. But as three Canadian teams made an unexpected run in the Stanley Cup playoffs, it was also obvious that no matter what decisions are made by those who control the business of the game, the passion for Canada's game remains.

⌒

THE BUSINESS OF the NHL is a 12-month proposition. Even as the players are enjoying their brief vacation, even as the Stanley Cup champions are savouring their victory, the scouts, coaches and general managers are preparing for what is the real beginning of their working year: the amateur draft. On one afternoon, the best 18-year-old hockey players in the world are divided among the NHL teams in the sport's version of redistribution of wealth. The worst teams, the most needy teams pick first, unless in their desperation they've already traded that choice away.

It's hardly an exact science. Looking at teenage players and trying to project how they'll fare as professionals is to some degree a crap shoot. The early first-round busts are nearly as numerous as those who were overlooked until late in the draft and developed into superstars. It's tough to predict how 17-year-olds or 18-year-olds might develop, what they might become, to take into account not just their abilities, but the context in which they've been demonstrated, the stage of development at which they were exhibited. To judge all of that and the person too – his level of maturity, his character, his work ethic – to understand how he'll perform after the money starts rolling in, after he's made it in the big leagues, even the greatest scout can't do with 100 per cent certainty. It's science to a point, and then it's an educated guess.

Still, around some players there develops a consensus, a conventional wisdom that suggests that so many pairs of eyes seeing the same thing can't all be wrong. In June 1997, when the draft was held at the Civic Arena in Pittsburgh, such a player was Joe Thornton. The big, blond native of St. Thomas, Ontario, knew he'd be the first player chosen overall long before he made the trip south. This was the most heralded hockey prospect to come along since Eric Lindros was chosen by the Quebec Nordiques (and then decided he didn't want to play in Quebec).

As a 15-year-old playing Junior B hockey in his home town south of London, Thornton had been visited by Wayne Gretzky's agent, Mike Barnett of the International Management Group; Barnett eventually became Thornton's agent. In his first year of Junior A with the Sault Ste. Marie Greyhounds – the team Gretzky had played for – Thornton put up 76 points in 66 games. In his second year, he had 41 goals and 81 assists in just

59 games. Though he wouldn't turn 18 until nearly a month after the draft and still had two years of junior eligibility left, the betting was that he'd become the first 17-year-old to be picked first overall since the Buffalo Sabres selected Pierre Turgeon ten years before. Thornton had originally said that he planned to go back and play one more year of junior, but if the Boston Bruins, who held the first pick by virtue of having the worst record in the league the season before, did indeed select him as everyone expected, most observers believed he'd have a real chance to stick in the NHL. He had size – 6 foot 4 inches, 198 pounds – he obviously had a scoring touch, and he had a bit of a mean streak. A more aggressive Gretzky, they called him, or a Lindros with better touch. Lindros had recorded 75 points for the Flyers in his rookie season. Many expected Thornton to make the jump and do much the same.

The NHL's Central Scouting Bureau, which produces talent evaluations for all of the league's member teams, had this to say about him as draft day approached: "Good skater . . . speed . . . balance . . . excellent puckhandling skills . . . vision of the ice . . . creates open spaces . . . powerful shooter . . . accurate passer . . . a finesse player who possesses a tremendous amount of aggression . . . has the ability to dominate a game . . . mentally tough . . . an unselfish player with a very strong work ethic . . . a team leader."

Dave Mayville, the general manager of the Sault Ste. Marie Greyhounds, was willing to go even further beyond the boundaries of the rink. "He has time for everybody. If there is a fault with him, that's probably it, but that's what makes him so special."

The Bruins, who had just completed a season in which they missed the playoffs for the first time in 30 years, were in desperate need of a superstar. They had the option of trading the first choice for an established player or two – especially since they also had the eighth pick in the draft by virtue of an earlier trade. But this was to be the beginning of a new era in Boston hockey – by necessity. Team president Harry Sinden, who had always shown a preference for hiring coaches close to home – coaches he could easily control and didn't have to pay too much, his critics contended – broke form and hired Pat Burns, formerly the man behind the bench in Montreal and Toronto. Burns was a high-profile, big-ticket hire, and certainly nobody's stooge. His arrival was a clear signal that the Bruins were serious about going in a different direction, that they were no longer content just to make the playoffs every year without taking a serious run at a championship. They had plenty of seats to fill in the new Fleet Center, the state-of-the-art arena that replaced tiny, decrepit Boston Garden. The fans had grown cynical. Grand gestures were in order.

And so there was no way they would do anything but use that first choice to sign the player who was supposed to be head and shoulders above anyone else in the draft, who had already been tabbed as the game's next superstar. By the time they arrived in Pittsburgh on draft day, the Bruins already knew that Thornton was their man. "We were very, very happy about it, getting the number one player," Boston general manager Mike O'Connell said. "It was a tough situation to go through to get that [finish last overall], but we were very happy. We picked a good year to have a bad year."

As for their number eight pick, the Boston hierarchy was open to suggestion. Two players particularly intrigued them – Daniel Cleary of the Belleville Bulls, a scoring star in junior hockey who had once been touted as a possible first overall pick, and a young Russian forward named Sergei Samsonov, who had spent the previous season playing alongside pros with the Detroit Vipers of the International Hockey League in order to improve his marketability after beginning his career in his

In his one season in the International Hockey League, Sergei Samsonov had enjoyed great success. But NHL clubs considering his worth in the 1997 draft worried about his size in a big-man's league.

native Russia. In the IHL, Samsonov had often dazzled with his skills and his poise and had shown no difficulties adapting to the level of play. He won the IHL's rookie of the year award, with 64 points in 73 games, and a standout +33 rating. In the playoffs, as the Vipers were winning a league championship, Samsonov played in all 19 playoff games and recorded 19 points.

Putting up those kinds of numbers in a league several steps higher than junior hockey suggested that Samsonov was a blue-chipper, a prospect ready to step right into the NHL and become a solid two-way player, perhaps even a star. Or at least it would have if Samsonov had been just a little bit bigger. Listed at 5 foot

8, 184 pounds, and perhaps not even that tall, he might be too small to hold up to the physical rigours of the NHL. For every undersized player who has succeeded among the giants of the modern game – Theo Fleury, for instance – there are dozens of others who possess the necessary skills to thrive even in the high minor leagues, but simply can't cut it in a league more and more dominated by size and strength. Samsonov would surely be a solid first-round pick, but one with an asterisk attached. A team might decide that even without overwhelming physical tools, he could be one of those small player exceptions, and gamble on him with a high pick. Or clubs selecting in the first ten might decide that they couldn't afford to gamble. They'd use their pick on a rawer talent, but one with the size and strength to handle the tough going of the NHL.

In order to help make up their minds, the Bruins, like other NHL clubs, conducted pre-draft interviews with the players, a chance to assess their character and temperament, a way to flesh out the scouting reports into something approaching a por- trait of the whole human being. "I can remember when Sergei walked into the room," O'Connell said. "I was tired, it was round four o'clock, it had been a long day, and Sergei walks in. It was funny, because Sergei was our last interview, and every- one we had brought in was six-two, six-three. And I look over as this kid walks in and saw that he was built – whereas the other kids were skinny and thin. I looked over and asked the scout, 'Who's this?' He said that's Samsonov. It really caught my atten- tion, the size of him. Not that he's a huge kid. Just that you see this guy walk in with all the square inches on him already. . . .

"The question I asked Sergei which I'll never forget was when I alluded to the finals that year, Philadelphia versus Detroit. I said, 'Sergei, did you watch any of the games?' And he said, 'Yeah, I watched the games.' I said, 'Could you play? You're five-eight. Can you play in that kind of environment where it's rough? You saw how physical it was. Can you play in that?' I remember he looked me right in the eye and he said, 'I've always been one of the smallest players on my team.' I had a feeling that his next words were going to be 'And I've always been one of the best.' But he caught himself and he said, 'I've always been able to get through it and play hard.' And that was the key moment in the interview process. It convinced me. That plus seeing him walk in, seeing how sure he was of himself as opposed to Cleary. Daniel was very nervous and this kid was sure of himself. There was no question he thought he could play in the National Hockey League."

The interview cinched it, and the Bruins had their game plan. Draft the big can't-miss-kid first, and then take a chance on Samsonov. The only question was whether someone would beat them to the punch.

· ↄ

ON DRAFT DAYS, there are often trades aplenty. Sometimes, a club will go against form, against the accepted hockey wisdom, and pick a player that no one expected. And sometimes, as in 1997, the proceedings go pretty much according to form. There would be no blockbuster trades. No shocking choices. Even those who wanted desperately to deal found a shortage of takers.

Mike Milbury, the general manager of the New York Islanders, arrived in Pittsburgh with two high first-round picks, the team's own at number four after missing the playoffs, and at number five the choice they'd acquired in a trade with the Maple Leafs, part of the deal that sent Wendel Clark and Mathieu Schneider to Toronto. The Isles badly needed help at centre and on left wing, but knew they wouldn't necessarily get what they were looking for at four and five. It was assumed by all that the best three players, all centres, would go in the day's first three picks – Thornton to Boston, with San Jose and Los Angeles following by choosing either Patrick Marleau of the Seattle Thunderbirds of the WHL or Finnish centre Olli Jokinen. After that, the next best choice seemed to be a goaltender, Roberto Luongo of Val d'Or in the Quebec Junior League. With Eric Fichaud already being groomed for the starting job and Tommy Salo under contract, goaltending wasn't a priority for Milbury's Islanders. Neither was defence, where Eric Brewer of Prince George was regarded as the next best prospect.

So Milbury arrived on the arena floor, where each team had a table, looking to make a deal – to trade one or both of his picks for first-line talent, or to trade down in the first round and pick up a useful body in return.

When the first three teams were picking exactly as expected, Milbury realized that the latter course was his only option. He'd try to swap the fifth pick for a later first round choice, and hope to get some third-line help in the bargain. The Tampa Bay Lightning held the seventh pick in the draft, and their president, Phil Esposito, had quietly expressed interest in moving up. Understanding their common ground, Milbury and Esposito entered into casual conversation, a kind of pre-negotiation. The fans sitting in the arena seats, waiting in vain for something dramatic to happen, might not have noticed, but Al Coates, the general manager of the Calgary Flames, certainly did. His team held the sixth pick and coveted Barrie Colts' centre Daniel Tkaczuk (the Bruins had feared that they might take Samsonov). Worried that Esposito might move ahead of him and select Tkaczuk before he had the chance, Coates asked his assistants whether they ought to make a pre-emptive strike – offer Tampa Bay a later round choice in return for not making the deal with the Islanders.

Meanwhile, Milbury broke off his chat with Esposito to step to the podium to announce his first choice. "To all our fans back

Holding two high first-round picks, Mike Milbury (left), the New York Islanders' general manager, looked for a possible deal with Phil Esposito, his counterpart with the Tampa Bay Lightning, shortly before the start of the 1997 draft.

in Long Island," he said, "we hope you're enjoying this day as much as we are. We're proud to select with the fourth selection, Roberto Luongo from Val d'Or."

Suddenly, the Islanders were rich in bright young goaltending prospects, richer even than they might have preferred. After taking time for the traditional photo opportunity, where the player dons his new team uniform for the first time, Milbury headed straight back to Esposito – pausing for just an instant at Coates's table to ask him whether they might have something to discuss. He could just as easily swap picks with the Flames. Coates said no, so Milbury moved on.

The Islanders brain trust had decided that in exchange for swapping picks with Tampa Bay, they wanted left winger Jason Wiemer. It was now up to Milbury to close the deal.

"You want Wiemer?" Esposito said, whispering behind his hand. "Anybody else besides Wiemer?"

"Wiemer was the guy we had our hearts set on," Milbury said.

Sensing Esposito's reluctance, he upped the ante. "I'll do more. I'll throw in something else."

"Who else?" Esposito asked.

Milbury paused. "We'll talk. I'm going to take a time out. We're going to milk this for all the TV time we can get." The time out allowed the Islanders to delay announcing their selection with the fifth pick.

Returning to the Islanders' table, Milbury conferred with his staff. "Would you guys give up [left winger Paul] Kruse? Wiemer is going to be a third-line guy ahead of Kruse anyway, so that wouldn't bother me a bit. Would you give up [defenceman Jason] Holland?"

Kruse, they agreed – Kruse and the Islanders' number five pick for Wiemer and the Lightning's number seven. Back went Milbury to the Tampa Bay table.

"Do you guys like Kruse at all?" Milbury asked Esposito.

"Not really, no."

"How about a pick?"

"What kind of pick?"

"We get Wiemer, and I'll give you Dallas's third rounder [which the Islanders had acquired in an earlier deal]."

"I don't think so, Mike," Esposito said. "We've got to keep Wiemer. The new owners want to keep him. That's why I wouldn't want to trade him."

Rebuffed and out of options, Milbury headed back to the stage. "I hope those fans on Long Island don't destroy us for [picking] another defenceman," he whispered to Bettman.

"With the fifth pick in the 1997 draft, the New York Islanders select Eric Brewer. . . ."

"That's exactly how I wanted things to unfold," Coates said

at the Calgary table, knowing that he'd be able to select Tkaczuk. "That's no bullshit."

·ᴗ

BY THEN THE DAY'S marquee moment had long passed, and what it lacked in suspense was made up for in part by the fact that a future superstar was being unveiled, perhaps not a Mario Lemieux or a Wayne Gretzky, but someone who would put his name in the record books, and perhaps add his name to those engraved on the Stanley Cup. It was no surprise to anyone when Harry Sinden walked to the podium to announce that the Bruins would choose Thornton first overall. Thornton came to the stage, accepting the congratulations of well-wishers, looking every bit the big, slightly awkward teenager with surfer-boy blond hair, and slipped into a black and yellow Boston jersey with his name on the back. Here was the next one, the player who would define hockey stardom for his generation.

It was more of a surprise – a very pleasant surprise for the Bruins – when Samsonov was still around to be chosen with the eighth pick, as Esposito opted for Sudbury defenceman Paul Mara. O'Connell breathed a huge sigh of relief. Big smiles all around. Then off to the stage to announce their choice, to confirm that the draft had played out exactly as they'd hoped.

When his name was called, Samsonov hugged his parents, who had left their life in Russia to follow him to Detroit as he pursued an NHL career. Walking to the podium, he smiled a nervous smile, but looked terrified at the attention. Finally, climbing the stairs, he was greeted first by the commissioner.

"Congratulations," Bettman said, shaking Samsonov's hand. "Welcome to the NHL."

One long journey had ended, and another was about to begin.

As expected, the highly touted Joe Thornton (left) was selected first overall in the 1997 draft by the Boston Bruins.

THE LIVES of both young men would change dramatically that day in Pittsburgh. Interest from the sports media, which they had known to a degree playing junior hockey, or in Samsonov's case in a minor league, would increase tremendously. Suddenly they would be confronted by cameras, by video cameras, by strangers carrying notepads and tape recorders, wanting to know the details of their lives, where they grew up, what teams they followed as boys, who their hockey heroes were, how they planned to help the Boston Bruins return to the glory of the Bobby Orr–Phil Esposito years. They would be asked about contracts, about money, about what their expectations might be. They would be asked larger questions about the game and their place in it, about what it felt like to be labelled the next Lindros, what it felt like to leave Moscow as a teenager in search of a very different life as a North American professional athlete. For teenagers, short on real world experience, that's a tall order, which is why so many young professional athletes fall back on a bashful smile and as many clichés as they've managed to master.

The happy truth, of course, is that suffering through a few stupid questions is part of what they get paid for – and, in the case of Thornton and Samsonov, paid rather handsomely considering they had never played a game in the NHL. Thornton would sign a contract that would pay him a base salary of $925,000 U.S. a season, the rate set in the players' collective agreement with the league for those drafted with the first ten picks of the draft. That cap was a reaction to the enormous amount of money the Ottawa Senators threw at Alexander Daigle when they drafted him first overall and represents the one instance in which hockey salaries are effectively held down. But creative agents have found that the rookie cap can be circumvented using incentive clauses. In Thornton's contract, six benchmarks were written into the deal: finishing in the top five in voting for the Calder Trophy, given each year to the league's best rookie; recording 20 goals, or 35 assists, or 60 points; having a points-per-game average of .73 or better; having a plus-minus rating of 10 or better. In the relatively unlikely event that Thornton hit two of the six marks – unlikely only in that so few 18-year-olds, no matter what their abilities, can make the jump directly from junior to the NHL and produce at that rate – his salary would jump to $2.5 million. Perhaps those figures wouldn't have seemed extraordinary if another organization had drafted and signed Thornton. But the Bruins and Harry Sinden had earned a reputation for thriftiness over the years. The fact that they, too, were willing to spend so freely left other NHL general managers shaking their heads.

"We are guilty of behaving in the same manner that many, many teams behave with their players," Sinden explained later. "We were going to sign those players no matter what the consequences."

Samsonov and his agent, Jay Grossman, took their cues from Thornton's contract, understanding that a number eight pick is not a number one pick, and that Samsonov certainly didn't have Thornton's star value heading into the draft. Initially, the Bruins weren't willing to match the incentive clauses, forcing Samsonov and Grossman to take a calculated risk. He would go to training camp, unsigned, and try to prove on the ice that he deserved the chance to earn every dollar

"When Sergei came along, Grossman said, 'We want the same as Thornton,'" O'Connell says. "And I said, 'No, I'm not going to give you the same as Thornton.' I mean, Thornton was the first pick overall, blah, blah, he was highly touted, the most highly touted player since Lindros. You know we're not going to sign for that. And he said, 'Sergei's going to come to camp and you'll have to pay him what you're going to give Joe, because he's going to dazzle you. And I said, 'Well, I guess we'll see.'"

⌣

HOW, ANYONE IN A normal wage-earning situation might ask, could a person be worth that much, let alone a hockey player, let alone a 17-year-old hockey player who had never done anything to establish his value to his team? And what was happening to this sport? Fans had become used to the astronomical salaries in baseball, where free agency – hard won by the players over the course of several labour wars – had been a reality for 20 years. They were becoming used to it in basketball, where individual players clearly had star power beyond the sport, and where one athlete of the five on the floor could make the difference. They had seen it in the National Football League, where even though the players' union was crushed the only time it dared to go on strike, where a salary cap was supposed to keep wages under control, each year brought another astounding set of numbers.

But hockey had been different. Wages had increased steadily, though not as dramatically as they should have, during the years when Alan Eagleson ran a players' "association" – not a union – in cozy concert with the owners. The last few seasons, with Bob Goodenow heading the Players Association, have produced dramatic hikes. The bargaining agreement between the players and the owners, signed in the wake of the 1994–95 lockout, certainly didn't seem like a radical document at the time. Allowing hockey players to become unrestricted free agents at age 31, 13 years into their professional careers, hardly compared with the market leverage available to baseball players, who can file for free agency after six. But even with limited mobility, the combination of unprecedented growth, expansion opportunities, a significant U.S. network television deal with Fox, and especially the arrival of deep-pocketed corporate ownership in the United States, drove the salary spiral higher. Each new standard, whether it was the Ottawa Senators' (unwise, in hindsight) rookie pact with Daigle, the Anaheim Mighty Ducks' offer that finally ended Paul Kariya's holdout, the offer sheet from the Carolina Hurricanes that forced Detroit to make Sergei Fedorov a very rich young man, or whatever Eric Lindros might command from the Philadelphia Flyers or another employer, was clearly temporary, with no end in sight.

There are obviously two conflicting viewpoints on salary escalation. For the players and their agents, what's not to like? Every season the bar is raised a little higher, every year hockey salaries creep closer to the stratospheric levels already found in other professional sports after years of lagging far behind. And of course, no one is putting a gun to the owners' heads and forcing them to pay. After years of being held back, even as the owners raked in profits, the players see their increased prosperity as evidence that the game is thriving. "Suggesting that the amount of money the players are earning is bad for the game would be improper; it would be foolish to say that," says Don Meehan, one of the most powerful agents in the game. "If you're an owner or a manager, you simply don't have to pay the players. If it didn't make sense, you wouldn't pay them. And yet they're paying them all."

The opposing viewpoint comes from the other side of the negotiating table – especially from those who operate the league's lower revenue franchises. There is an enormous difference between the financial realities faced by the Disney-owned Mighty Ducks of Anaheim, or the New York Rangers, and their small-market cousins in Edmonton, or Ottawa, or even Long Island, at least if you believe Islanders' general manager Mike Milbury.

"I have to have a salary structure that reflects my own economics," he says. "We are not the New York Rangers and we are not the Philadelphia Flyers. We're in desperate need of a new building. Our attendance has been down – for good reason. The team's not been good. But just because Viktor Kozlov is going to get two million or Daniel Alfredsson is going to get two million, I don't care if their statistics are identical to one of my player's. It doesn't make economic sense for me."

But of course if Milbury won't pay market value, someone else will. And that market value will be established not necessarily by anything he does, but by a decision some other general manager made about another player, allowing an agent to draw comparisons. It is the game of "comparables," and there's no better example than the negotiations that led to enforcer Tie Domi signing a new contract with the Toronto Maple Leafs.

In the spring of 1997, the Leaf organization was in an even more chaotic state than usual. The hiring of former goaltending great Ken Dryden as president of the franchise seemed like the dawn of a new and better era for a team that hadn't won the Stanley Cup since 1967. But with Cliff Fletcher's departure, the club was also without a full-time general manager. Bill Watters, a former player agent and former radio personality, had been Fletcher's assistant. While Dryden pondered over whom he might hire as GM (he eventually settled on himself, with Mike Smith as his chief second), the operation of the team, including the signing of players, was left to Watters.

In what would turn out to be his last act as interim general manager, Watters took on the task of negotiating a new contract with Domi. A tough guy with some hockey skills, Domi had won a place in the hearts of Leaf fans because of the way he used his fists and because of his obvious work ethic, one of the few bright lights in an otherwise disappointing season that had cost coach Pat Burns his job. Domi's agent, Don Meehan, understood that Domi's popularity in Toronto gave him added value in the marketplace. At such a crucial stage in team history, the Leafs surely wouldn't risk the fan reaction they'd face if they let him leave. But at the same time, how much could a player like Domi possibly be worth? What's the market value of a player who does his best work with his fists rather than his stick?

Watters decided that Domi was worth, at most, a million dollars a year. But Meehan had other ideas. He would use a negotiating technique that really dates back to a conversation in the Detroit Red Wings dressing room decades before. Bobby Baun and Gordie Howe were talking salaries – something Howe had never done with his fellow players. Mr. Hockey was shocked to learn that Baun was making more money than he was. He soon found out that a whole lot of players were making more money than he was, that Detroit management had lied to him even as he was setting scoring records and winning Stanley Cups.

From that moment was born the concept of "comparables." The players – and more importantly, their union, the National Hockey League Players Association – came to understand that the more salary information was shared, the better. One player's raise would pull other players along with him. In negotiations, agents would only have to cite "comparables" – other players in essentially the same category as their client who were making more – in order to justify asking for similar amounts of money. Now, all salary information is shared among the players and their agents, with the understanding that such knowledge is power.

"It's easy to sign a player if you just give them what they want," Harry Sinden says, expressing how the owners feel about comparables. "When they ask you for it, you give it to them, you've got your player signed and you're a hero. But there's another [concern], to fight for what's fair and what's right and to keep your team profitable. Part of what you're doing as a manager is managing the owner's money. So if you start listening to comparables around the league, where people don't care about that, then you too will be in the position they're in. . . . They have a 35-goal scorer making $8 million. So is that a comparable for our 35-goal scorer? I don't think so. Not in negotiations."

Sergei Berezin is a Russian winger, a finesse player who was supposed to inject some much needed scoring punch into an anemic Maple Leaf line-up. In 1996–97, his rookie season, he scored 25 goals, suggesting the high hopes of the organization were justified, that Berezin was the real thing.

Still, aside from the fact that they wear the same uniform, what could Berezin possibly have in common with Domi, an entirely different kind of hockey player, at a different stage in his career, who played a different role? You'd be surprised.

During the summer of 1997, Toronto Maple Leafs' acting general manager Bill Watters (left) and player agent Don Meehan (right) crunched numbers in the contract of Leaf enforcer Tie Domi.

Consider this, the actual conversation between Meehan (along with his associate, Pat Morris) and Watters, conducted by speaker phone, as they haggled over what Domi was worth to the Maple Leafs. Watters did his best to sound tough, to occasionally sound angry. Meehan kept the same measured tone throughout – all posturing, since both men understood that they wanted to make a deal, and that it was in Domi's interest and the team's interest to keep him in Toronto. But at what price?

MEEHAN: "It's very difficult for us to bring a player in, to look the player in the eye and say, 'You played here eight years and the Maple Leafs have paid a player between a million seven and a million eight. He's been here one year and he had 41 points and you had 28.' And I've got to tell him that you're saying to me that's outrageous. I can't pay you $1.5 million. You have to tell me why that's outrageous."

WATTERS: "Berezin and Domi are not comparables. With all due respect to both parties, they are not comparables. If you are going to compare Domi to Bob Probert . . ."

MEEHAN: "Bill, Bill, are you telling me that 41 points to 28 points, there's no relevance?"

WATTERS: "I'm talking about the type of player involved and the need that he fills. If you want to stick to the 28 over 41, then let's make a deal."

MORRIS: "I'll stick to this, Bill. Tie Domi had 25 even-strength points, Berezin had 29. It brings the distinction down to four points when they're on the ice on a five-on-five basis."

WATTERS: "Twenty-eight is to 42 – it's 41 – but 28 is to 42 as four is to six as two is to three. Unless we're going to drop the Berezin story, let's stick to the numbers."

MEEHAN: "No, no. I'm not prepared to let you just draw the distinction or the analogy on 41 to 28, because what you're doing, Bill, is to ignore the 275 [penalty] minutes."

WATTERS: "Look at my line-up. We'll find somebody who can get 275 minutes. I don't want it to get to that, Don."

MEEHAN: "I know, but I don't want to have to be [in your shoes telling] the Toronto community that you'll get somebody else to do it as well as he does it."

WATTERS: "Do you think Gino Odjick doesn't do it better than Tie Domi or as good?"

MEEHAN: "No, he doesn't. Pat Quinn would take Tie Domi at the drop of a hat. You know that as well as I do."

WATTERS: "That's not the function here. The function here is to make a deal. You want $1.5 million, you're not going to get it. I want a million, I'm not going to get it."

MEEHAN: "Bill, I've known you too long and I know the Berezin deal hurts you people as a comparable. One guy got 41 points, one guy got 28 points. The guy who got 28 is a regular, he's the best at what he does in the league today and you're saying to me he should take $600,000 less."

WATTERS: "He doesn't have to take anything."

MEEHAN: "I know, but he's not going to. As much as you

can say to me you know we're not going to pay it, you've got a problem on your hands because you've set a precedent on Berezin. Like it or not, he's there."

Three weeks later, after further haggling between Watters and Meehan, Domi didn't get his $1.5 million. He got an average of $1.43 million over five years, far more than Watters had said he was willing to pay. (Asked afterwards, Watters said he felt justified in paying that much because of the long-term nature of the deal – it included an option for a sixth year. By the end of the contract's term, he figured, salaries will have escalated so much that Domi will look like a bargain.)

Back in Meehan's office, the agent tried to explain to his client why they had failed to secure a million and a half dollars a year. Meehan's tone was vaguely apologetic, even though the figures were astronomical by any measure.

MEEHAN: "There are some GMs, when they get wind of this number, there's going to be havoc. Seven million one hundred and fifty thousand dollars for five years. Now that breaks down to $1.43 million a year. Pretty close to that $1.5 million that we felt it would take to do a year. It's very much like Berezin. He starts at $800,000. He goes to $1 million. He goes to $1.2 million. He goes to $1.4 million, and then he goes to $1.75 million plus $400,000 in signing [bonus] in the fifth year."

Then the agent changed tack, gingerly addressing the topic of why Domi was being paid all that money. He fights, in a game where fighting has value. And enforcers, at a certain point in their career, often decide that they no longer want to do what got them there in the first place. Meehan wanted to make sure that wasn't the case with Domi.

MEEHAN: "Now there's another thing that we haven't talked about today. There probably hasn't been an individual like you who does what you do that at a certain point in time loses a real zeal to do that. It doesn't become so much fun. And it's not easy what you do. And that's why you're commanding this kind of money. . . ."

Pat Morris jumped into the conversation.

MORRIS: "When I was driving into the office today I had occasion to speak to Craig Hartsburg, and I said . . . if we could deliver Tie Domi [at] about $1.435 million, what would you say to that? He chuckled and he said I'd say yes, in a heartbeat, run to it. Run to it."

MEEHAN: "We wouldn't have a chance in hell of getting these numbers with 99 per cent of the teams in the league. But we do, due to your own strength, how popular you are in this community."

Through all of this, Domi didn't say a word. He looked grim, ferocious, as though he were about to square off with Bob Probert. For the longest time, after Meehan finished his pitch, he remained silent. Then finally he piped up with his first words in the discussion.

DOMI: "This is all U.S.?"
MEEHAN: "Yeah."
DOMI: (laughing) "We still have this same thing, this same fifth year, guaranteed?"
MEEHAN: "Yeah."
DOMI: "And the sixth year is an option like the fifth year?"
MEEHAN: "The sixth year is talking about $1.9 million."
DOMI: (beaming) "Let's get it done!"

After listening to an explanation of a new multi-million-dollar deal by his agent, Don Meehan (with Meehan's associate, Pat Morris [left], looking on), Tie Domi (right) simply beamed and declared, "Let's get it done!"

The look on his face is the look of someone who is thrilled to be playing hockey for a living, who probably never expected to have a shot at the NHL, who would certainly do it for a whole lot less than $1.43 million – U.S. – a year if he had to, if not for nothing. And he can't quite believe that he's been lucky enough to make more money than he ever could have imagined.

"The media are going to have their say, the fans are going to have their say," Domi said later. "If everybody thought like I do, I think everybody in the whole world would be rich. Because I'd be happy for anybody, it doesn't matter who it was, to sign contracts or people who win the lottery. I'm happy for anybody. It's a short life and you've got to take advantage of everything when you can get it. I'm in one of those situations where, hey, I'm the happiest guy in the world."

IN HOCKEY, as in all other professional sports, the days when training camp was the beginning of a player's conditioning program are long gone. By the time they report for medicals, NHL players, after enjoying a brief summer vacation, have already begun the process of building themselves up for the long season. In some cases, that pre-camp preparation has become nearly as elaborate as training camp itself. Young clients of the IMG agency spend three weeks at the Minnesota Hockey Camp, the brainchild of Chuck Grillo. In 1997, Joe Thornton and Daniel Cleary, both first-round picks, were there, as well as Drake Berehowsky, a former first-rounder who found himself without a contract. Under Grillo's supervision both in the gym and in the classroom, they tried to prepare themselves to win jobs in the National Hockey League.

For the veterans, the stars, those secure in their employ-ment, it's simply a good investment in their greatest asset – their bodies. For young players, or those on the bubble, there is of course added incentive. Training camp and the exhibi-tion season are their chance to win a big-league job, to begin earning big-league money. In order to do that, they'll have to make an impression, to demonstrate during practices and scrimmages and whatever limited ice time they receive during game conditions, that they belong – and by extension, that someone else doesn't belong. Looking down the row of lockers in a camp dressing room, every player knows that if he's to make the team, several others will have to be let go, sent back to juniors or down to the minors. There is camaraderie among the players, but certainly not what it will be once rosters are set and the season begins.

Of course, it's not just the players who understand that careers in professional sport can come to a sudden halt. Across the league, coaches go to camp knowing that their security depends entirely on taking the talent they've been given and fashioning it into a winner. With some teams, the stakes are far higher. In 1996–97, the Philadelphia Flyers advanced to the Stanley Cup finals, only to lose to the Detroit Red Wings. That wasn't enough for ownership, or for general manager Bob Clarke, who fired coach Terry Murray. Former assistant Wayne Cashman, who had never run a team in the NHL, was handed the reins and a clear mandate: win the Cup, or else. In Montreal, young Alain Vigneault assumed what many consider the most pressure-packed job in all of professional sports, coaching the Canadiens. He arrived in the wake of a disappointing season, which was followed by the emotional departure of Mario Tremblay. To ease his entry into the job, the Habs also hired an extremely capable right-hand man – veteran coach Dave King. In Buffalo, both coach Ted Nolan and general manager John Muckler had been dismissed after feuding through the final weeks of what had been an extremely successful season for the franchise. Darcy Regier assumed the GM's post, and Lindy Ruff took over as coach, knowing that his dressing room was deeply divided over Nolan's ouster, that the team was in the process of being sold, and that the club president, Larry Quinn, was on shaky ground. In Toronto, the story was a familiar one: without much talent, coach Mike Murphy would try to lead the storied franchise back to respectability. "We didn't make the playoffs last year," he told his players on the opening day of camp. "This year we're going to make the playoffs. That's the simple goal." In Vancouver, the addition of Mark Messier was supposed to make the Canucks a Stanley Cup contender – and it was coach Tom Renney's and general manager Pat Quinn's job to make sure that happened. Even in Detroit, where they were still celebrating a Stanley Cup victory, where coach Scotty Bowman had all of the security seven championships can bring, there was the challenge of dealing with the tragic off-season traffic accident that had left defenceman Vladimir Konstantinov seriously brain-injured.

In Boston, following the worst Bruins season in a long, long time, the message was clear: this is a new coach, this is a clean slate, there are no guarantees, no assumptions. All jobs are open. Opportunities abound. "There are openings here that only present themselves once in a while," Harry Sinden told the players, "and it's here on this team this year."

Included in that equation, of course, were Joe Thornton and Sergei Samsonov. In another organization at another time, Thornton, for all his press clippings, would face the real possibility of being returned to junior. For Samsonov, that obviously wasn't an option, but still the prospect of a minor league assignment would have been very real. Instead, both young players found themselves on a team rebuilding from the ice up, prepared to take chances, to carry a rookie and live with his mistakes in return for a payoff a few seasons down the road. Both players would have to be exceptionally disappointing in camp to play their way off the team.

Still, they had Pat Burns to impress, a coach who can be tough on young players, and whose own considerable paycheque was based on winning games, not babysitting prospects. In that, Samsonov had the upper hand from the very first workout. Just as his agent had predicted, he dazzled with his speed, his skills, his playmaking ability. He showed no hesitation around the veteran pros, and despite his lack of size, he wasn't easily intimidated, or shoved off the puck. The year of seasoning in the IHL had obviously paid off, and the Bruins' hierarchy could start congratulating itself for seeing what the six teams who passed on Samsonov might have missed.

"He's a quick little bastard, isn't he?" Boston general manager Mike O'Connell said to team president Harry Sinden, sitting in the stands watching Samsonov in a scrimmage.

"Nice play. Jesus Christ what a play! Did you see that play?"

That performance would earn him a contract nearly identical to the one Thornton had signed.

"It's a tribute to Grossman that he knew his player," O'Connell says. "He knew his player, he knew what he could do, what he couldn't do, and he was willing to bring the player to camp before a contract was signed, when a lot of other agents wouldn't."

Still, all of the encouraging signs from Samsonov couldn't make up for the fact that Thornton, their prized number one pick, seemed lost. He shied away from physical play. His scoring touch betrayed him. "He gets his chances all the time and he misses all the time," O'Connell said to Sinden. "He misses the net." He looked less like a Gretzky or a Lindros, and more like any number of early picks who were huge disappointments, at least in the early days of their professional careers. Chatting privately with Sinden, O'Connell made reference to one of them – Jason Allison, a first overall pick by the Washington Capitals in 1993 who hadn't lived up to expectations before being traded to Boston the season before where, as it would turn out, he would blossom into a first-line player.

"I was saying to Cheesey [Gerry Cheevers], we should take a film of Allison and show it to Thornton and say this is what you're going to be if you don't get your . . . act together."

"He wasn't prepared," O'Connell says of Thornton now. "He didn't know what to expect. . . . Sergei had an idea of what it was going to be like. Joe thought he had an idea, but he didn't. He didn't realize these guys were this much bigger, he didn't realize that the American League players were as good as they were. He didn't realize that guys from out of college can skate and shoot, just like guys out of junior.

"Let's face it. Joe's been told from probably the age of 16 that he's going to be the next guy. He goes to junior, he plays terrific in junior, does all of those great things in junior. Now he gets into his first pro camp, and it's like yeah, I'm good, but there are a lot of good guys here. And I think he was probably a bit surprised by the calibre, not only of the players who are stars in the National Hockey League, but players who played two or three years in the minors and who are fighting to get into that position."

The press was critical of Thornton's performance in camp. Coach Pat Burns made it clear that he wasn't the kid's biggest fan. But this was a Boston team without great expectations for 1997–98, and Thornton was obviously the key to their long-term plans. If he could get enough ice time with the Bruins, perhaps his NHL seasoning ought to begin right now. Or they could send him back to junior. For Sinden, for O'Connell, it may have been their toughest choice on the eve of the season. Send Thornton down and acknowledge that the guy everyone had painted as a can't-miss superstar wasn't yet ready for even third-line duty in the National Hockey League. Or keep him around, throw him into the deep end, aggravate the coach, and take the chance that the pressure, the fan and media criticism that was sure to come his way, would have a devastating effect on the young man's confidence. A hockey life, and a huge investment, hung in the balance.

"We were going to do everything we could to make these kids make the team, because we thought that we might not be a very good team with these guys in October/November," O'Connell explained at season's end. "But if these guys can learn, progress, come January and February, they're going to be a big part of this team. So we were all on the same page. We talked to Pat extensively about this before we even hired him. We told him, we're going to have a young team, Pat. You've got to be patient with us, we'll be patient with you, and let's bring these players along. And he did, he did. . . . Pat was very easy to deal with on both players. He knew they were good kids, they worked hard. He knew Sergei was a little more prepared for what lay ahead of him and he knew Joe was going to have some kind of attitude adjustment. This is a business. There are 20 guys on this team and 19 know it's a business. Joe, you've got to start realizing that it's a business, too, and make it 20."

· ⌒

IT IS OCTOBER, opening night of the 1997–98 season. All teams are equal. All teams still believe, some with more reason than others, that eight months from now, they'll be the ones celebrating a championship.

Tie Domi, new contract in hand, is on the ice for the Toronto Maple Leafs, ready to earn his pay with his skates and his stick and his fists. Sergei Samsonov is in the line-up for the Boston Bruins, after a training camp in which he proved that he belonged.

Joe Thornton is sitting and watching from the press box. During an exhibition game, he'd been slashed on the hand, breaking a bone. Any decision on his future would have to be delayed until the injury healed.

The puck is dropped. The cycle begins anew. The Cup is up for grabs.

Sergei Samsonov (centre) rewarded the Bruins for gambling on him as the eighth pick overall in the 1997 draft by winning the NHL's Calder Trophy as the league's top rookie.

Joe Thornton, the kid who couldn't miss, struggled through his rookie season as a Bruin. A broken bone in his hand landed him in the press box with his father.

· FOR THE GOOD OF THE GAME ·

To BE WANTED is a wonderful thing. For the game of hockey as played in the National Hockey League, there could be no greater confirmation of its ascendance into the ranks of top-drawer North American professional sport than the fact that cities were clamouring to join the club. Not traditional hockey cities, since the only ones still without teams were in Canada, and the league wouldn't be expanding in that direction any time soon. These were places where the sport had little or no history, where most people had never played the game, and many had never even seen it. But hockey was big-time, it was big-league, it could put a city on the map – at least that's what they'd been told. Civic boosters and sports fans alike figured it was worth whatever price had to be paid.

It hadn't always been like that. When the NHL first expanded beyond its traditional six-team base for the 1967–68 season, it was a mixed success. The game took tentative root in Philadelphia, St. Louis, Pittsburgh, Minnesota and Los Angeles, but foundered in Oakland, where the California Golden Seals died a lingering death. After that, the St. Louis Blues would almost wind up being moved to Saskatoon. The Minnesota North Stars would eventually be shifted to Dallas. The Kings would struggle to attract fans in Los Angeles. And the Pittsburgh Penguins would occasionally teeter on the financial brink. Only the Philadelphia Flyers, the first of the new teams to win the Stanley Cup, would have an essentially untroubled history.

35

Subsequent efforts to expand the league's reach were similarly problematic. The first foray into the Deep South – the Atlanta Flames – eventually became Calgary's team. The Kansas City Scouts/Denver Rockies/New Jersey Devils took forever to find a home. The clear message seemed to be that hockey was a regional game, and a regional game it would remain. In Canada, in the U.S. northeast, the fans understood its nuance, and the sport could find a niche. Outside of that, and especially in the U.S. sunbelt, it might never break through.

That might still be the case but for the events of 1988, when Peter Pocklington's personal financial difficulties forced him to make a decision that would forever earn him the ill will of Edmontonians. He sold Wayne Gretzky to Los Angeles, cutting a deal with the Kings' flamboyant new owner, Bruce McNall. The greatest player in the game, its greatest star at the height of his powers, would be shipped to the largest market in the United States, a place where NHL hockey had hardly made a dent during its 20 years of existence.

Having Gretzky in Hollywood changed everything. The seats at the Forum were filled, movie stars staked out prime spots along the glass, Kings stories suddenly appeared on the front of local sports sections and led the television sportscasts. It was the idea of Gretzky they bought into, not the fine points or the legacy. It was the notion that the absolute best at something was plying his trade in their town. Pure star power, pure celebrity. Suddenly, hockey had sex appeal in a place where before it had barely existed, in a place where veneer was all.

The Kings would never win the Stanley Cup with Gretzky. McNall would have his own financial problems and wind up in jail for swindling banks. Hockey in Los Angeles would eventually fall back to being just about what it was before the Great One arrived. But what Gretzky begat could be seen all across the United States. A second California team thrived in San Jose, just up the road from where the Seals had been such a colossal failure, and then a third popped up in Anaheim, under the Disney banner. Hockey became a solid attraction in Texas, where football had previously been the only sport in town. In Florida, two franchises were immediately successful. Hockey had crossed the sun barrier. It was no longer a purely regional attraction. Move over baseball, football and basketball. Make room for one more.

Gary Bettman, the commissioner of the NHL, would ride that wave. His job was to exploit that new popularity, to push the sport's growth while demand was at a peak. Further expansion would dilute the talent pool (as it does in every sport), and at least temporarily would hurt the product. But all teams would share in the expansion fees, and all owners would see their franchise values boosted by the activity of the open market. Hockey was hot, and it was time to strike.

And so, on to Nashville, Tennessee. Say the name, and hockey certainly doesn't spring to mind. Nashville is country music, it's the Grand Ole Opry, it's the South. In sports terms, it has historically been not much of anything, although it shares the statewide passion for college football.

But Nashville had become more aggressive than any other city in North America in courting professional sports franchises, seeing that as the key to growth and to enhanced civic identity. The city would pay whatever the price, it would build the facilities and offer sweetheart rental deals, it would do whatever it took. When the Houston Oilers of the National Football League were looking for a place to move, Nashville offered to build a 65,000-seat stadium, part of a $292-million, publicly funded "relocation package." The Oilers took the bait. And in 1995, the city constructed a 20,000-seat arena, and offered $20 million to any NBA or NHL team willing to relocate there. Both the Hartford Whalers and New Jersey Devils took a look, using the threat of a move to extort better deals back home. (The Whalers eventually moved to Carolina in any case.) When the NHL decided to add four teams by the year 2000, expanding the league from 26 to 30 franchises, Nashville found itself near the top of the list, willing and able and rich. Eleven groups from nine different cities (including a token bid from Hamilton, Ontario) vied for the franchises in June 1997: Nashville along with Atlanta, Columbus and Minneapolis-St. Paul were the winners of a prize that would cost each of them $85 million.

There was only one catch. In order to secure the franchise, local fans were told by the NHL that they'd have to put down deposits for 12,000 season's tickets. Even some cities already in the league didn't have that kind of guaranteed fan base, and the fact was that the NHL had never been put in the position of turning down an expansion application from someone who could write the cheque for the team. It could be reasonably assumed that a small shortfall in sales might be conveniently swept under the rug.

Still, a little threat was a nice way to kick-start a marketing campaign in the virgin hockey territory of Nashville. Would-be owner Craig Leopold, who had made his personal fortune in the rainwear business, underwrote a slick marketing campaign for the team, unveiling a flashy, sabre-toothed tiger logo even before the team officially had a name. At the kick-off event for the season's ticket campaign, Leopold told the crowd that he'd been receiving many letters of support from local fans, including one that particularly hit home.

"There's one individual whose name is Martin, he's ten years old and he's a huge hockey fan."

Leopold then read from the letter.

"Mr. Leopold. I'm a long-time hockey fan with some suggestions on how to jump-start the franchise. Number one.

*Growing the game, or diluting it? Rainwear magnate Craig Leopold bet
$85 million U.S. that the NHL belonged in Nashville.*

Choose the name the Nashville Predators. Ice Tigers sounds
stupid and Fury is just plain stupid. Number two. Find some great
marketers, and continue the strong marketing push. Your team
will not step onto the ice unless 12,000 season's tickets are sold."

Leopold broke away from his reading.

"He actually said it and he's right."

Then back to the letter.

"Respectfully, Martin.

"P.S. Keep the ticket prices low the first year then raise them
later."

Predators it would be. Leopold then commissioned a series
of television commercials, some featuring stars of country music
extolling the virtues of the game in twangy voices, others
designed to explain the nuances of the foreign sport to the
locals. The latter featured a character called Professor Boom
Boom, who spoke in a stereotypical French-Canadian accent
and taught his students the game on a rather basic level.

"Point number one – Shoot that puck, and score that goal."

"Point number two – If the other guy has a different colour uniform, you knock him down."

By such methods, the Fastest Game on Ice would find itself a new audience. The subtleties they'd pick up over time.

⌁

SITTING AT HIS CUBICLE in the St. Louis Blues' dressing room after a game in January 1998, speaking his mind as he is wont to do, Brett Hull simply said what so many others were thinking. The son of the legendary Golden Jet, Bobby Hull, Brett Hull is one of the National Hockey League's superstars, a gifted scorer with a blistering shot. Because of his famous last name, because he was an American citizen who had played for the United States when they'd won the World Cup, Hull was also one of the league's most important marketing tools. In an era in which games are sold through the star power of individual athletes (an approach perfected by the National Basketball Association with Michael Jordan), Hull was much more than just another player.

And so when he said, "The game sucks," a lot of people, beginning with the reporters crowded around him for a comment to fill out their stories for the next morning, were going to listen. "I wouldn't pay to come watch it," Hull continued. "It's boring and it's not a whole bunch of fun to watch. There's no flow to the game at all. As soon as a team gets going, you just ice it or throw it out of the building. Something's got to be done with our game."

How would he fix it? Hull was asked.

"I don't know. That's not up to me. But they've got to do something."

And why hadn't something been done already?

More "brain lock," or words of wisdom? Shoot-from-the-lip NHL star Brett Hull rattled the league by declaring, "The game sucks," after a game in January 1998.

"Probably because the wrong people are in charge."

He couldn't have imagined it at the time – in any case, Brett Hull isn't the kind of person who chooses his words for effect – but that post-game statement sent shock waves throughout the NHL that continued for the 1997–98 season. While what he'd said was brash and ill-timed and spur of the moment, it also rang true to those who loved hockey. The great, free-flowing, fastest game on earth, as personified by the Edmonton Oilers of the 1980s, and by so many great teams of the past, had been replaced by something else. Teams playing a negative, defensive style found ways to neutralize more talented, offensively minded teams. Phrases like the "neutral zone trap" and the "left wing lock" crept into the hockey vocabulary. Hockey fans might not have understood the technicalities of the strategy, but they knew the effect: to slow the game to a crawl, to turn what used to be thought of as interference into a legitimate coaching tactic. Check opponents to a standstill. Grab and hook and do anything you can to slow down the play-makers, to keep the scorers away from the puck. Test the referee's tolerance every night, and do whatever you could get away with. And when all else failed, ice the puck, or freeze it, or flip it into the crowd.

For disciplined, well-coached teams, the strategy worked. It took the New Jersey Devils all the way to a four-game sweep over the apparently more skilled Detroit Red Wings in the 1995 Stanley Cup finals. It took the Florida Panthers, just three years old, all the way to the Stanley Cup finals in 1996, where they finally lost to the Colorado Avalanche.

Very talented teams, like the Wings and the Avalanche, could still overcome. But for any coach who didn't have that calibre of players, for any coach of an expansion team or in the midst of a quick rebuilding process or hoping to save his job by making the playoffs, playing the negative game was incredibly tempting. Do it and a superstar could be neutralized by a bunch of middle-of-the-road players. Do it and the most talented team wouldn't necessarily win.

Gretzky and others had complained about it. When he retired in 1997, still near the peak of his powers, and again when he was inducted into the Hockey Hall of Fame in the fall of that year, Mario Lemieux had talked about the frustrations he'd faced during his final seasons. He said that he could no longer handle the on-ice abuse, that he no longer had the desire to fight through the holding and hooking, all of which was technically illegal, just to do what he was paid to do. It wasn't the only reason he quit, but the fact remained that the sport lost one of its greatest attractions in part because it had decided not to enforce its own rules.

During his state-of-the-game message, Hull also took note of that. "When a guy like [Lemieux] leaves the game and tells you why he's leaving the game and you don't address it, that's stupid," he said. (Hull also had something to say about the very expansion process that the people in Nashville were so excited about: "Expansion makes it worse. It dilutes the product, and now they're going to expand the game.")

For coaches and general managers, the aesthetics of the sport were distinctly secondary to victories, since it was victories that secured their employment. But for the fans, the paying customers, and especially for those who had some sense of the game's history, of what it could be at its best, the new, defensive style made for terrible entertainment. Many a night during the long and often apparently meaningless regular season, they were in the arenas or at home in front of their televisions and saying to themselves exactly what Hull had said, no matter how much it might have pained them to say it: "The game sucks."

It didn't take Gary Bettman long to understand that Hull's words weren't simply going to fade away. Across Canada, and more importantly to the commissioner, across the United States, even in places where the NHL had not yet become a presence, the story was recycled again and again: variations on the theme "Star Player Rips His Own Sport." All of those slick promos, all of the Fastest Game on Ice T-shirts, all of the time and effort spent on selling hockey in places like Nashville didn't mean a whole heck of a lot if a player came out and said he wouldn't buy a ticket to watch it. That wasn't just the whining of some Canadian purist. That was a shot directly at the product. Something had to be done.

Bettman's first instincts, understandably, were towards damage control. For politicians and business leaders and sports commissioners in a bind, denial with an explanation is the natural first course. Muddy the waters a bit, offer up some vaguely plausible excuse, and hope that the public buys it. It was a strategy that Bettman would employ again a few weeks later, when things went awry at the Nagano Olympics.

"I spoke to Brett Hull yesterday myself," Bettman said to reporters, "and Brett told me that he regretted the comment. He attributed it – and these aren't exactly his words, but they're close enough – to brain-lock. Once in a while Brett gets quoted saying things that people find outrageous, such as we should boycott the Olympics and a whole host of other things. On reflection, I don't think he meant those comments. At least that's what he said to me."

But give the commissioner credit: he understood that wasn't going to be enough. He understood that Hull's words wouldn't be forgotten. And perhaps he understood, deep down, that there was truth in what Hull said, that there was a problem with the game, with the product, a problem he, the team owners, and those who actually shaped the game – the general managers – were going to have to confront and correct.

·⌣

THE ANNUAL MEETING of NHL general managers was held in 1998 in beautiful Scottsdale, Arizona, sandwiched in time between Brett Hull's outburst and one of the most important events in the history of the league, the showcasing of NHL pros in the Olympics at Nagano, Japan.

In the meeting room, the commissioner had the floor. Away from the press, away from the public eye, Gary Bettman sounded a very different note than he had in public in the aftermath of Hull's comments. The measured tones of his performance in front of the press, the calm veneer he likes to maintain no matter what the circumstances, changed with the audience. Now he was talking to general managers representing the 26 NHL teams, many of them former players, but none of them particularly sympathetic to a player's right to speak his mind. They were angry about what Hull had said, and in a mood to shoot the messenger.

*At the 1998 annual meeting of NHL general managers, held shortly after
Brett Hull's outburst, league commissioner Gary Bettman faced a roomful of
executives furious with Hull.*

"We're trying to sell this game," Edmonton's Glen Sather had
told the meeting. "I don't understand how we can let our players
do what they do to our game. They make all the money, and if
there's something wrong with it they magnify it."

"We're just asking for their help," said Mike Milbury of the
New York Islanders. "We want to go forward and sell the game
and put it in the best possible light."

The commissioner didn't bother trying to convince them
that Hull hadn't really meant what he'd said, that he'd had
"brain-lock," that it was all an innocent mistake. Those lines
he saved for reporters and the paying public. Here, he just
sounded mad as hell.

"I've got to tell you," Bettman said, "I haven't had to deal
with this much damage control on very many things to this
extent. We're out there trying to sell tickets. We're out there
trying to make sure our ratings are strong enough. I've seen the

*"We're trying to sell this game," Edmonton's Glen Sather complained to his
fellow general managers in the wake of Brett Hull's broadside.*

video of the sports shows of the last three days and the media
around the country – we've got a real problem. We've got a real
problem in terms of the perception of this game right now."

The only person in the room willing to defend Hull was Bob
Goodenow, president of the National Hockey League Players
Association, who also had a seat at the table. A former player
agent, the union leader was a far stronger advocate for his membership when dealing with management than had been his pre-
decessor, the disgraced Alan Eagleson. Eagleson would be the
first to attack players who stepped out of line, but Goodenow
rose to Hull's defence.

"It's not like Brett Hull – though we know he's outspoken,
he hasn't come out and ripped the game in the past," he said.
"I know last night he was at the Hall of Fame at the King Clancy
Dinner [an event to benefit charity]. He does a lot of things to
promote the game on balance."

But Bettman wouldn't be placated, and he wasn't about to be conciliatory, especially in front of a roomful of hockey executives.

"My point is – and I'm using this as an example for you and for all the managers – it's important that we understand the damage this kind of statement can cause," he said. "Because you know what, this game doesn't suck. This game isn't boring."

"Let's put it all in the proper balance," Goodenow said, trying to calm the waters. "I hear what Glen's saying. No one condones it or is happy about what happened. But we have to go forward and we have to deal with the issue. That's what I think this meeting's about."

Bettman then moved beyond Hull-bashing and into the broader context of public relations. The best chance for the NHL to get past the Hull controversy came with these meetings and the message they would send at their conclusion.

"We're not talking about Brett now," the commissioner said. "What I'm trying to get everybody focused on is that the media, as it tends to do, is very focused on this meeting and what comes out of it. We have an opportunity to come out of this with all of you – and I include you in this, Bob – saying the right things about our game so that we can move forward and get out of this morass that we find ourselves in, where people are bashing the game."

And of course, the game was everyone's bread and butter – general managers, players and the head of the players' association alike. They might be on different sides of the table come contract time, but in a larger sense, they were all part of the same business, and all in the same boat. Sounding a conciliatory note, Goodenow was willing to acknowledge that.

"It's a lesson for everyone," he said. "We don't need to have that kind of statement made public. Especially when all that gets picked up and relayed across America is: 'The game sucks, the game sucks.' We do have issues that need to be discussed, and sometimes it can prompt us into looking at them."

There was the key – not to leave it at that, not to vent their frustration with Hull and with players in general and then to pretend everything was fine. Though they might have avoided the issue in the past, or discussed it and then didn't follow through, this time the NHL's power brokers didn't leave it at what Hull had said and how he shouldn't have said it and how other players had better not say it in the future. They did all of that, and then they looked in the mirror and said, maybe he's right. Maybe we do have a problem. Maybe the game, the product, isn't what it ought to be. Maybe it isn't what it was, and it isn't what we're selling to people. Maybe it's time for a change.

In the world of professional sport, that spirit of self-criticism is as uncommon as a kind word from management for a player agent. The National Hockey League had acknowledged, privately, that it had a problem, and it set about trying to fix it. All that took place during the course of a day and a half during one remarkable meeting.

· ᴗ

THE NATIONAL HOCKEY LEAGUE'S rule book already contained everything needed to solve the problems of the game that Hull had outlined. Hooking and holding, the main sins perpetrated against puck carriers, are already prohibited. So is interference, which in the broadest terms is undue contact with any player who isn't in possession of the puck. Call all of the penalties that ought to be called, and the goal scorers wouldn't be impeded, the play-makers would have free reign. But at the same time, if you called all the penalties that ought to be called, the defenders might not have a chance, and in any case, power plays would come to dominate the game.

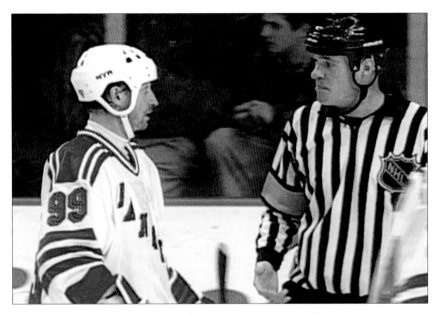

Wayne Gretzky argues for a penalty after teammate Mike Keane is downed. Inevitably, every NHL referee operates with a series of personal biases, and there are differences in styles of refereeing.

That's why referees' discretion became a part of hockey in the first place, and why its officials still have the power to influence individual games more than the refs and umpires in any other sport. Every NHL referee operated with a series of personal biases that were as individual as a baseball umpire's strike zone – and players and coaches came to understand that a Kerry Fraser–refereed game was going to be different than, say, a Paul Stewart–refereed game. That had been the case in hockey as long as anyone could remember, and in some ways the strong personalities of its officials were part of the show.

Though no one in a position of authority would ever admit it, referees were also expected to exercise their judgement beyond what it said in the rule book, to take the game situation into account when making a decision. Calling it by the book was reserved for regular-season games that didn't mean a whole lot, when it was deemed necessary to send a get-tough message to the coaches and players. A close game would be called differently than a lopsided game. In a tightly contested, more meaningful encounter, when one team was given the man advantage – especially on a borderline or questionable call – a penalty often seemed to go the other way almost immediately, just to even things up. In the part of the year that mattered most – the Stanley Cup playoffs – it was almost as though an entirely different set of standards applied. A game would be called by the book in the first period. A little more would be allowed to pass in the second. Then, in the third or in overtime, only the most grievous foul would result in a power play. No one wanted a key game, let alone a championship, to be decided by an official's call.

The players, the coaches, everyone understood the system, understood the personalities, and any deviation would result in howls of protest. During those times when the league occasionally tried to crack down on one type of foul or another, when the referees were instructed by their superiors to call the game in a different way, there would invariably be all kinds of carping. And just as invariably, the get-tough spirit would last only so long, with the game and officiating eventually reverting to form. For instance, back in 1994, the general managers met just as they did in 1998 and called for a crackdown on restraining fouls, just as they would in 1998. Whatever changed didn't change for long.

"Every year that I've been coming to these meetings we talk about the same things," said Phil Esposito of the Tampa Bay Lightning. "The people change but the subject doesn't."

The difference, this time, was the acknowledgement that there was a problem – enough of one that the paying public and the press were starting to notice, that the criticism by Hull and Lemieux and others was eventually going to have an effect

Brian Burke, the NHL's senior vice-president of officiating, bore the brunt of criticism over inconsistent penalty calls.

at the box office and on television revenues. Of course, not every NHL general manager shared that opinion. Though bound by hockey, they were a diverse group, some former players, some former coaches, some front-office lifers, some conservative, some progressive, some locked in tough-guy mode, some more genteel.

This would be a debate, an argument of pros and cons, with the opening premise: let it be resolved that something is wrong with our game.

"Those penalties should be called," said Neil Smith, general manager of the New York Rangers, the team that employed the most skilled player in the history of the sport, Wayne Gretzky, who had also taken more abuse – legal and illegal – during his career than anyone before or since. "The game would be better, and the scoring would go up. I don't think that many of us during our 82 games are very happy at the end of the game with the officiating."

That statement struck a nerve with one person in the room. Brian Burke, the NHL's senior vice-president, was in charge of the league's officials and was also the one who doled out discipline – suspending coaches or players who went beyond the bounds of acceptable behaviour. Like many a high school vice-principal, Burke was cast in that tough-guy mould. Any criticism of NHL officials was an implicit criticism of the way he'd been doing his job.

"I couldn't disagree more, Neil," Burke said.

"That's fine because you're not a GM," Smith said. (Burke had been a general manager, with the Hartford Whalers, and would be one again before too long, taking over the reins of the Vancouver Canucks.)

"I know I'm not a GM but I felt the same way when I was a GM," Burke said, his voice rising in anger. "I felt we lost [fair and square] a lot of nights. I didn't think the ref screwed us when we lost."

"I miscommunicated if that's what you heard," Smith said, trying to turn the discussion away from direct criticism of the referees. "Because I didn't mean that they're not good. The officials *are* good. But the way they're calling the game under our instructions is what I meant. That's what I'm trying to communicate."

The question then was what should the officials be told? What kind of instructions were they being given, and what kind of instructions should they be given? How should the game be called and how strictly should the rules be enforced? What kind of change was necessary? Bobby Smith, general manager of the Phoenix Coyotes and a skilled play-maker during his long NHL career, put the issue on the table.

"Are we allowing the best players to be brought down to a level of mediocrity of the really unskilled guys?" he asked. "And maybe more importantly, are we totally eliminating the opportunity for a guy who's not a great player to score?"

Anaheim Mighty Ducks star Teemu Selanne (centre) is one of the skilled players who gets rough treatment. Phoenix general manager Bobby Smith asked, "Are we allowing the best players to be brought down to a level of mediocrity of the really unskilled guys?"

Bettman picked up that theme.

"There are a lot of games where the puck carrier, particularly some of our more skilled players," were being badly abused, he complained. "And is that okay? Or should we be looking at that as well in terms of the standards that we're giving the officials? I mean, do we think we're letting the puck carrier take too much abuse?"

All of that was just a little bit too much for Mike Milbury to stomach. Despite his years behind the bench and in the executive suite, Milbury remained at heart the player he had been with the Boston Bruins, someone whose work ethic and desire made up for any shortfall in talent. He also bore the stamp of the Boston organization and his former boss, Harry Sinden, who didn't suffer prima donnas, who preferred to build around hard-nosed grinders rather than finesse players. A team full of Milburys would need every advantage they could get, within the rules or otherwise, to deal with the league's superstars.

He wouldn't mince words.

"Some of these new-age players who can't take a hit – screw 'em," Milbury said, approximately. "We haven't been any-where near as physical in this league in terms of hitting. And all I hear from these dick players is, oh my god they're hooking me, they're holding me. Screw it. Shoot the puck. Work hard. They're spoiled."

"What the public wants is the aggressive puck carrier," Smith said. "And he's being withheld illegally. Either he's hooked, he's pulled down, or he's slashed in the shoulder. He's slashed in the elbow, he's slashed in the hand. I agree with Mike Milbury that if it's a legal check, you can take him out. But should we allow the stick up around the elbows? Around the waist? Let him take slashes? He's earned his role with his abilities. Now we're letting it be taken away by players *with no abilities*."

Bettman then brought the discussion back to the rules, and more importantly to their enforcement.

"This isn't about passing a new rule. It's about calling this one right. How much physical abuse? What's the standard? And if the standard's the one we've got and everyone's in agreement, fine. But if we're not calling it tight enough in terms of pro-tecting the puck carrier, let's discuss it."

The next to enter the fray was Bob Clarke, general manager of the Philadelphia Flyers. During his career with the great Philadelphia team known as the Broad Street Bullies, Clarke and his cronies were known for bending, breaking and utterly ignoring the rules in order to intimidate their opponents and win hockey games. Their style defined the 1970s, a time when it seemed to many that the sport had reached a low ebb. As a general manager, though, Clarke had built a very different kind of team, a team for the 1990s, featuring the player who was supposed to dominate the decade, Eric Lindros. Lindros could certainly look after himself on the ice, with his combination of size, strength and occasional bad attitude. But he was also a play-maker and scorer who could be made a whole lot less effective if the opposition was allowed to clutch and grab.

"We're letting the obstruction get out of hand again," Clarke said. "That's all. It's a lot easier for a skilled player to play if the guy he goes to pass to isn't being knocked on his ass. You can't be checking people who don't have the puck. The puck is the game. And we get away from that. We forget all about the puck. There are six or seven players on the ice in each . . . shift who could care less that the puck's out there."

But was that all the referees' fault, or was it the fault of those who were telling them how to call the game?

"I believe that one of the areas we should revisit is the fact that they're not calling any marginal calls," said Pierre Gauthier, general manager of the Ottawa Senators. "I think when we told that to the officials, what basically happened is that we moved the threshold of what's being accepted, and from that point they just put the whistle away. And that's what we're running into now. A lot of stick fouls on the puck carriers."

Clarke was quick to jump to the officials' defence.

"In my opinion, other than the obstruction that's going on, the refereeing is better now than it's been in ten years," he said. "Way better. But we get in a group like this, and pretty soon one guy's got an idea that initiates a thought in someone else's mind. Now we all think that we've got to call more penalties – let's get more penalties in the game, let's get more power plays, let's get more five-on-threes. I mean it's . . . crazy. It's a great game. Fix up the obstruction. Let the players play a little bit. You say we shouldn't hook the guy with the puck too much. Well, a little resistance towards a guy scoring isn't so bad either. Let's not make it so damn easy that just because a guy's got skill he's going to waltz through the whole . . . team like they do in kids' hockey. It's men playing hockey. That's what we want to see."

It would seem to be a fine line – call enough obstruction penalties so that the skilled players could strut their stuff and entertain the fans, but don't call it tight enough to really interfere with the nature of the game. Give the defenders a chance, make the players play like men. Don't make it too easy for the scorers, but don't make it too hard. The game's not broken, but fix it – a little bit.

The next step would be to try to communicate that to the officials and their supervisor, Brian Lewis, to tell them what they were doing wrong and tell them how to make it right. From afar, the games looked one way. Up close, on the ice, with the sound of the players and the coaches and the crowd in your ears, it was reasonable to assume that they looked a little different. Still, if change was going to come, it wasn't going to come through the rule book, but rather through its interpretation. It would be up to the referees to carry that out.

⸱᷄

BLAMING THE REFEREES for the state of the game is a little like blaming Brett Hull for saying what he thought – in this case, not shooting the messenger, but shooting the employee. The refs work for the NHL. Brian Lewis takes his cue from the league's head office, and especially from the league's general managers, who are the authoritative voice when it comes to rules and regulations. They are given guidelines under which to call the games, and then go out and try to follow them. Each has his own idiosyncrasies, but that's always gone with the territory.

When Lewis was called before the general managers in Arizona, it was clear from the outset that he was on the hot seat. It was clear from watching games on videotapes that there were numerous examples of obstruction penalties that should have been called, but weren't.

"The standard was extremely high and I think that we got away from it a little bit," Milbury said. "I don't believe the standard from where we started the obstruction rules is the same as it is today."

"I can guarantee it is not," Lewis said. "Statistically we're not bad. But game by game, when we break them down and analyze them as you people do, we have to sit there and say we're not pleased."

"Why do we get away from that stuff [calling the obstruction penalties]?" Sather asked. "The attitude of the referees has all of a sudden shifted to where you can go ahead and take this guy out, it's legal. I don't understand why it gets changed. Who changes it?"

"All of us here want the obvious calls called," Lou Lamoriello of the New Jersey Devils chimed in. "That's what we're talking about."

Lewis, understandably, became defensive at that point. It wasn't that simple. The calls weren't that obvious. And many of the same general managers who were decrying all of the uncalled interference in the game were employing coaches and players who exploited just that strategy to win. When a referee called one of those infractions, the wrath of that coach, employed by that GM, would surely fall upon him. So whose fault was it, really, that no crackdown had been enforced?

"I think we're remiss just pointing the finger at the officials and saying you're not [doing this], you're not [doing that], when in fact a lot of it is a coaching tactic, a coaching technique. And the players are getting cuter," Lewis said. "That's why I say it's a tough one for all of us to accept because normally it's not one that we're all looking for."

There was some sympathy in the room for Lewis's viewpoint.

"Our game evolves every six months or every year," Glen Sather said. "We have a turnover in here. Our opinions change. You get some new referees. New linesmen. There's new coaching tactics. The game is always evolving. It makes it very difficult for the referees to understand the message that we want to get across to them. A lot of times those of us in this room don't even know what we're trying to tell them."

"Brian," Lamoriello asked, "from your perspective in the referees' situation, is it the intimidation from the players, is it the intimidation from the coach, is it the directions that we keep giving that are confusing, that they don't know where they are? What would you pinpoint as to why it isn't where it was?"

Lewis explained that the problem was that, whatever was decided during league meetings, whatever the general managers and coaches and players agreed to in principle, things changed during the hockey season.

At league meetings or during training camp, the players, the coaches and the referees were all on the same page. Then once the season began, almost every obstruction call was met with a complaint. Lewis suggested that if there was a new consensus among the general managers that the penalties would be called, and that they'd accept them, the referees would try again to enforce the rules as directed. But at that, Bettman snapped back.

"You know perfectly well it's been the consensus of everybody in this room and from Brian [Burke] and me for the last two years that we wanted this stuff called."

Lewis countered, "[What I'm hearing is] this is a great rule for 25 teams. Just don't call it on mine. At last night's game, I'm standing there and thinking, geez, that's a good obstruction call. But somebody's beating on the door and saying that's horse shit, how can you call that?"

There was also one other possibility, beyond whether the rules were written correctly, beyond whether the referees were enforcing them as they should. What if it was simply too much to ask one man in a striped shirt to control the modern game? Acknowledging that the task of officiating had become more difficult, the National Basketball Association had gone to a two-referee system. The NHL had maintained its traditional officiating crew of a referee, who could call penalties, and two linesmen, whose job it was to rule on offsides and face-offs. The notion of two referees might raise the spectre of twice the penalty calls, and twice the power plays – but if the game really had to be changed, at least some of the general managers thought that a more radical approach was worth considering.

"The rules are pretty good, aren't they?" Milbury said. "I think the changes we made were pretty good. But we've somehow got away from enforcing them. What I wanted to suggest – and what I've heard some of you guys say – is maybe this time we think about two officials and one linesman."

Bettman was certainly willing to entertain the possibility, but argued that the league should proceed slowly.

"Let's assume we thought going to two referees was a great idea," he said. "There are two issues. One is we've got to get through the rest of this season. Two, I think we've got to get a standard first. I'm increasingly of the view that it may be impossible for one guy to call this game. But what's the standard we want?"

Other, more radical changes were also brought to the table. What about eliminating the centre ice red line, returning the game to its original form and freeing up play in neutral ice? What about moving the goal lines out from end boards, creating more room behind the goal? What if we restricted the goaltenders'

Before the 1997–98 season was over, the NHL was preparing physical changes to the rink to open up the game. The AHL was used as a guinea pig, with the goal line moved two feet out from the end boards.

ability to handle the puck outside of the crease? What if we made the goalies' pads smaller? Wouldn't all of those measures open up the game for the skilled players as much as calling a few more holding penalties?

That kind of talk scared the more traditional thinkers around the table, who feared what might happen if the form of the game was altered too drastically or too quickly.

"I think it's a great game, and if we start meddling around too much with the rules we're going to ruin it," Sather said. "We can tinker a little bit with the rules. But we'd better be careful that we don't really do too many huge changes that really affect the flow of the game. It's guys like me, guys that are in the manager's position, that are thinking about the welfare of the game, that have to be strong and make sure that we don't let too many changes happen to it. But some modifications may be the right thing to do."

·ↄ

IN THE END, after a far-reaching, sometimes fractious, but in the end very productive debate, the general managers emerged with a series of recommendations.

"There are three things that we're going to work on from a league standpoint," Bettman said as the meetings drew to a close. "One is we're going to get a better definition of goalie equipment and make sure that it's purely protective and not defensive. Two, we're going to look at some system – probably two referees – we're going to look at some system for a differ-ent set of eyeballs calling penalties. The third, which we dis-cussed first thing, was having a zero tolerance on hands and sticks. And we're going to talk about the obstruction and inter-ference standard. Some of that we're going to implement after the Olympic break."

During the next pre-season, the league would experiment with eliminating the red line. "This probably isn't something we're going to do unless the results are so dramatic that we're all overwhelmed," Bettman said. It would carry out further trials by using the minor International Hockey League as a guinea pig. There, in some games, the goals would be moved towards centre ice, the goalie wouldn't be allowed to handle the puck behind the goal line, there would be no line changes allowed in the neutral zone, and minor penalties would have to be served for the full two minutes (rather than allowing the penalized player to return to the ice if the opposition scored a goal with the man advantage).

"If we adopt some or all of these, the sense is that we're going to pick up the pace a little bit," Bettman said. But there would be no rush to change, no immediate overhaul of the game. The consensus was that it wasn't broken so badly that it needed a quick fix.

The sport would be altered simply by having the referees call the games more closely, paying particular attention to obstruction penalties. The league pledged that this time, there would be no backsliding, that the decisions made in the meeting room would be carried over to the ice, not just for a few games or a few weeks, but for the rest of the season, the playoffs, and beyond.

And perhaps all of that would have happened even if Brett Hull hadn't had a bad night, hadn't had a bunch of reporters standing around him, hadn't shot his mouth off, hadn't spoken his mind.

Or maybe not.

·⁓

AS THE MEETINGS ADJOURNED, three final tasks remained that were nearly as important as the decisions that had been made. The first was to sell the rule changes, and the potential rule changes, to the hockey public through the hockey press. That would be Bettman's job, and the job of the general managers during the scrum with reporters after the final press conference. The journalists would be looking for an angle, for some sense of how the debate had progressed, and for some idea of how the sport was about to change. Was this a radical restructuring, or simply window dressing? Was it the same empty talk of years past, or had Hull's message – and the fans' dissatisfaction – actually got through?

Bettman, who has made a point of trying to understand how sports reporters think, made sure that the GMs understood the official spin before the meetings adjourned.

"These are all fine-tuning. We are not necessarily doing any of these. This group to a man likes the game and doesn't think we're falling off the face of the earth."

The hard-core fans had to be assured that the more radical suggestions – like the elimination of the red line – were unlikely to ever be adopted by the NHL, that they were purely experimental. The game wouldn't be turned on its head, and it especially wouldn't be turned on its head by the kind of American philistines who had named a team after a kiddie movie and who had brought the glowing puck to Fox Television.

"All of us from Canada are very proud of the game, very proud of the historical role that Canada has played in developing the game," Brian Burke said. "But my answer to the Canadian fan who says that you can't change too much about the game is we've got 26 GMs. I think three of them are American. So the rule changes are being guided by a largely Canadian group, and I think people can relax. . . .

"I think every league should look at its rule book every year, and if they can make the game better they should. But they should proceed with caution. If they can make the game more exciting, they should do that. But you have to remember that every time you change a rule to make one thing happen, it has an adverse effect somewhere else on the ice surface. In my mind that's the risk."

Meanwhile, it was left to Lewis to try to explain to his referees what was now expected of them, while not conveying the message that they were being blamed for the game's troubles (though to some degree, they obviously were).

"We must have a heightened sense of restraining tactics on the puck carrier," he told them, outlining how the GMs now wanted penalties assessed. "The stick between the legs is not a penalty. The defenceman in front of the net who puts the stick between the legs is not a penalty. But then if the guy in front of the net says, I want to go over here and forecheck and the guy takes him and spins him around, that becomes a penalty. Restraining tactics on the puck carrier must be called."

And finally, Goodenow, the union head, had to sell the changes to his membership, to convince them that it was all for the good. Getting that message across to the superstars, to the scorers and play-makers, to those who benefit most from a more wide-open game, would be no challenge at all. But the grinders, those who made their living slowing down the big talents, were also brother hockey workers. What Goodenow was telling some of those on the fringe, whose talent was just barely enough to keep them in the NHL, was that their days as big-leaguers were probably numbered.

"The whole point of it is to control the flow of the game," Goodenow said during a briefing session in the St. Louis Blues dressing room. "And this is where the focus of it is going to be. It's going to be phased in. The first phase-in point is going to be following the Olympics. The referees are going to be a little more sensitive and it's going to be notched up. It will start after the Olympics slowly, but then it's going to build, and next summer and next fall, it's going to come in full-blown."

Right after his speech, Goodenow quietly took Brett Hull aside. Here was the guy who in many ways had started it all, whose ill-chosen – or well-chosen, depending on one's point of view – comments after a game had set the process in motion. "The game sucks," Hull had said, and though the commissioner and the general managers had been ready to lynch him for saying it, they had obviously also taken his words to heart.

For his part, Goodenow just wanted to let a union member know that when the insults were flying at the general managers' meeting, the union president was there to stick up for him.

"When they were giving you the gears, I said, 'Hey now, wait a second. Hull has done a lot for the game. In fact tonight he's going to the [King] Clancy banquet.' It was perfect timing."

The changes were set to kick in immediately after the league paused for the Olympic Games in Nagano. There, hockey fans would be treated to a very different version of the sport, played on a large ice surface, free of fighting, where the skill players would have lots more room to manoeuvre. Ask just about anyone involved with the NHL before the Games, and they'd have told you that international hockey was boring by comparison to the North American game, that fans wouldn't ever warm up to the lack of body contact, to the lack of the physical intensity the small ice brings. After a couple of weeks of watching the Olympics, they would have told you, the fans would be happy to get back to their favourite teams and their favourite sport – with the rules tweaked just enough to make things a little bit better.

⸎

THERE IS JOY IN NASHVILLE. The slick marketing campaign, the season's ticket deadline, they've all paid off. They might not know hockey in Tennessee, they might not understand that the game is going through a crisis of confidence, but they know they like their Predators, and they especially like the feeling of being part of another big-league sport. In the end, it hadn't been easy. The Predators sold 3,000 season's tickets the day they went on sale in September. By January, they had sold only 3,000 more, which left them 6,000 short of their goal with three months to go. Professor Boom Boom's message apparently wasn't hitting home.

But the urgency of the artificial March 31 deadline worked wonders in the end, just as the NHL anticipated it would. A local car dealer offered a season's ticket to anyone who bought or leased a new car during a two-week stretch. A local grocery store chain bought 50 tickets to give away. One of the minority partners in the team, already on the hook for 20 per cent of the franchise fee, coughed up for 500 season's tickets. Members of the local corporate community had couriers arrive at their door in full goalie's regalia, handing out hockey sticks with a pitch to buy space in private boxes. Country music stars Tim McGraw and Faith Hill performed for the team at Ryman Auditorium, where bluesman Delbert McClinton debuted a little ditty called "Hockey Tonk – The Predators Song." A month before the deadline, a local television station staged a ticket-selling telethon.

All of that, the wave of community spirit, the desire for big-league recognition, and perhaps even a growing passion for hockey, did the trick. On March 28, three days before the deadline, the Predators announced that they had crossed the 12,000-ticket barrier. They were in. The National Hockey League had its 27th team. Nashville mayor Phil Bredesen, caught up in the excitement of the moment, proclaimed Nashville Predators Day. Majority owner Craig Leopold thanked the city, and then celebrated.

By then, the enforcement changes proposed at the general managers' meeting in February were already starting to take effect during the late stages of the NHL's regular season. More obstruction penalties were being called. The players were beginning to adapt to the new, tougher refereeing. The game was slowly but surely opening up.

It had to, more than ever. Because by then, the same hockey fans who had despaired at the decline of the sport had been able to watch ice hockey at its absolute peak, ice hockey in all of its high speed, freewheeling glory, just the way they remembered it.

Not in the NHL, though. Not in North America, not live in prime time, not in the way they'd expected. The Nagano Olympic tournament would be a revelation from start to finish, a surprise, a challenge to preconceived notions about who was who and what was what in the hockey world.

Most of all, it would prove that the game, when played as it could be played, certainly didn't suck, that it still could be the best entertainment in professional sport.

· GROWING THE GAME ·

THE RAILWAY STATION in Nagano, a nondescript indus-
trial town to the north and west of Tokyo near the snow-capped
mountains they call the Japanese Alps, is like nothing in North
America. Modern, spotlessly clean, it sits dead centre in the
city's downtown, next to a busy shopping district that is like a
miniature version of the capital's famous Ginza. Escalators take
passengers to the main waiting area, where they can buy tickets
both for local commuter trains and for the Shinkansen – the
bullet train that will whisk them away like the wind. Each
ticket comes with a number on it, a number coinciding to a place
on the downstairs platform. Stand on that spot, and when the
train arrives, on time to the minute, it will stop with one of its
doors exactly there. Step in, and you are where you're supposed
to be. Japan is like that, the future as imagined by children
watching "The Jetsons." It is a place of wonderful efficiency and
numbing bureaucracy in which decision making can take
forever. And even as the miracle trains whiz by, at the Zenkoji
Temple at the other end of the main shopping street, crowds
burn incense and perform the rituals of the ancient, living
Shinto faith.

This February morning was like any other at the rail termi-
nal, or at least any other during the 1998 Winter Olympic
Games, when Nagano was temporarily a hub of activity.
Virtually every bit of available space was filled with travellers,
Japanese and foreign visitors, lining up for tickets, rushing to

trains, buying hot canned coffee from one of the vending machines that are as much a mark of the country as pachinko parlours and sushi bars. The only thing out of the ordinary was a group of reporters and television cameramen, virtually all of them Canadian, the bulk of that country's journalistic crew sent to bring the story of the Olympics home. They stood and waited in the chilly open courtyard for the train from Tokyo that would, of course, arrive on schedule. They stood and waited for a moment of history to unfold before them just as surely as the trains would run on time.

Finally the players came up the escalator one by one, wearing the red jackets and caps that were the familiar uniform of the Canadian Olympic team – Olympians like any others, and yet like none before, at least in the Winter Games. Twenty of the greatest stars in the NHL including its greatest, Wayne Gretzky, were in Japan to represent their country in the first Olympic hockey competition that would be open to all players. Some walked through the gauntlet relatively unscathed. A few paused to answer reporters' questions before boarding the team bus. But for Gretzky, it wouldn't be so simple. He was mobbed, surrounded, the centre of a great mass of humanity that slowly moved through the station. Ron Maclean, Don Cherry's straight man on "Hockey Night in Canada," tried valiantly to fire questions while pinned to Gretzky's side. Railway security agents, used to the always orderly Japanese crowds, seemed unwilling or unable to step in and help. Through it all, Gretzky smiled the smile familiar to all hockey fans, to all Canadians, still the boy from Brantford after all these years, even after being sold to Los Angeles, after marrying a movie actress, after taking his show to New York. While those around him began to panic, he seemed to be thoroughly enjoying himself.

With all of the focus on the players, the real story of the day was easy to miss. It was in the reaction of the crowd, hundreds

Still the boy from Brantford: Wayne Gretzky smiled his way through a crushing reception at the train station in Nagano, Japan, as the most celebrated member of the Canadian Olympic hockey team.

of ordinary Japanese who just happened to be passing through the station at that moment. They had no way of knowing who would be arriving. Even if they had, it's debatable that they could have identified any of them, including Gretzky. The only universally recognized hockey player in Japan before the Olympics was Paul Kariya, the Anaheim star who is of Japanese descent and who had been marketed heavily in the weeks leading up to the Olympics. But because he had suffered a concussion before the Games, Kariya wasn't there.

Still, understanding that something out of the ordinary was taking place, the people stopped to watch. They stood against the station walls as the mob passed. Cameras were brought out, flashes popped. Teenaged girls giggled as though they were in the presence of a heart-throb pop star. They cheered and they waved and they followed the players to the bus, where Gretzky, the last to board, stopped to offer a nod and a smile.

By the end of the Olympics, they would surely recognize the greatest player in the history of the game. By the end of the Olympics, they would surely understand the star power of these athletes and the glories of their sport. They'd know the difference between a defenceman and a goaltender, between a Ranger and a Canadien and a Mighty Duck. They'd buy the T-shirts, the jerseys, the souvenir pucks, the videos. They'd watch the NHL games that would eventually become available on television. They'd buy their children sticks and skates and bring them to the rink. They would be converted.

This was only the beginning, the prelude to a master plan so brilliant that it couldn't help but succeed.

OF COURSE IT REALLY all began six years earlier, in the blistering summer heat of Barcelona. There the 1992 Summer Olympic Games featured the debut of what would be known as the Dream Team, an all-star men's basketball team representing the United States, made up of the greatest players in the National Basketball Association. In theory, the United States was sending pros because the college players who had represented the country in the past were no longer a sure thing to bring home a gold medal in what had been undeniably America's game. In fact, the Olympics represented an unprecedented global marketing opportunity for the NBA, something well understood by its president, David Stern, and by its executive vice-president, Gary Bettman, a bright young lawyer and one of Stern's acolytes. Basketball already had enormous international potential – only soccer is played more widely and in more countries. But being able to beam Michael Jordan and

Larry Bird into millions of households around the world would jump-start the globalization of the game, opening up a planetful of virgin markets.

The Dream Team's first Olympics did not turn out to be an entirely satisfying experience. The members stayed in a luxury hotel, far from the Athlete's Village, and arrived at their games in limousines. Playing against opponents who were in awe from the opening tip, they were never seriously challenged, running up enormous margins of victory without once appearing to be pressed. Watching the Americans destroy their opposition lost its novelty value almost immediately, even for the most jingoistic Yanks. And for those who still retained quaint notions of what the Olympic Games were supposed to be all about, the entire Dream Team concept seemed antithetical to those ideals. But it sold the NBA product, sold it brilliantly, and so, four years later, another group of superstars took to the court in Atlanta, with exactly the same result.

By then, Bettman had become commissioner of the National Hockey League and had already begun the task he had been handed by the owners – to sell the game, to expand its borders, to bring it closer to the big three professional sports – basketball, baseball and football – in the United States, to chart a marketing path into the next century. Globalization would necessarily be a major part of that. Having experienced first-hand the Dream Team phenomenon, Bettman set out to negotiate an Olympic showcase for hockey. Scheduling Olympic hockey would be more difficult, since the Games took place smack dab in the middle of the NHL's regular season. But it was also potentially far more rewarding, both for the league and the International Olympic Committee, which as a movement didn't need any more one-sided tournaments, and as a business depended for its livelihood on North American television revenue.

Basketball could produce one Dream Team. Hockey could produce six. Nevertheless, the presence of the Russians, Swedes, Finns and Czechs was largely beside the point, aside from providing tough, entertaining opposition. The real allure of having National Hockey League players in the Olympics was in the star power of those who would play for the Canadian and, especially, the U.S. teams. Though the American audience adored the Summer Olympics, where they knew their athletes would win more than their fair share of medals, the Winter Olympics had truly caught the country's imagination only once during the television age (not counting the Nancy Kerrigan–Tonya Harding freak show of 1994). That came in 1980, when an unlikely group of U.S. amateurs won the hockey gold medal in Lake Placid, New York, beating the mighty Soviet Union in the semi-final game before beating the Finns in the final. The Miracle on Ice became the stuff of legend, the stuff of Wheaties boxes, and a made-for-television movie.

How to push that button again? Perhaps with a U.S. pro team that would definitely not be an underdog, that had talent on par with any other nation on earth. The growth of hockey in the United States had been dramatically enhanced by the number of American players who were making an impact in the NHL, a fact that became apparent to all when the U.S. team won the 1996 World Cup. In an open Olympic tournament, their team would enter as gold medal favourites along with Canada, an enormous opportunity for the NHL to push its product in the few areas of the United States that were still resistant to the game. Beyond that, there was potential for growth in Europe, and especially in Japan. The host country had in the past shown itself willing to embrace foreign sports, and of course any league that could capture even a tiny fragment of the market share would stand to reap enormous rewards. For the National Hockey League, for the Olympic

Games, for the television networks, it seemed like a no-lose proposition.

In Canada, an open Olympic tournament would have an appeal beyond any marketing concerns, but culture and history surely weren't factored into the decision to take the NHL to the Games. Canada had won six of the first seven gold medals awarded in its national sport, the last coming in 1952 in Oslo, when the Edmonton Mercurys beat the best the rest of the world had to offer. After that, the brave bands of amateurs proved no match for the teams of the Soviet Union, which employed its athletes year round as hockey players though they retained their "amateur" status in the eyes of the Olympic movement. Canadians eventually were soured on Olympic hockey, soured on the hypocrisy of the amateur hockey establishment, and dreamed of the day when we would finally be able to send our best.

Those years of frustration culminated in the greatest sporting moment in Canadian history, the 1972 series in which an NHL all-star team eked out a victory over the Soviets on Paul Henderson's goal of a lifetime. Subsequent series went back and forth, establishing in every Canadian's mind the fact that supremacy in hockey, while still a possibility, could never again be taken for granted. In games played in our rinks, on our timetable, our best were usually better than their best – as evidenced in the Canada Cups. But in games played overseas, on the larger ice surface favoured in Europe, all bets were off.

There remained one unknown, one patriotic flashpoint, a forum in which we were never given the opportunity to show our stuff: the Olympic Games. Even after professionals began making an appearance, Canada had little chance to win gold because the best players in the world were locked up by the NHL schedule during the Olympics. In 1992 in Albertville, a team featuring a teenaged Eric Lindros lost to the former Soviets in the final, settling for silver. In 1994 in Lillehammer, a team led by Paul Kariya, who had yet to sign with Anaheim, and Petr Nedved, in the midst of a contract holdout, came even closer, losing to Sweden in a shootout in the gold medal game. But what if Gretzky had been there? What if Mark Messier had been facing down Peter Forsberg? What if Patrick Roy or Curtis Joseph had been in goal, and Al MacInnis had been firing slap-shots from the point? Who would have won it then?

Even in 1994, other hockey countries could have said the same thing, since so many of their stars were also employed in the NHL. But only in Canada would winning a gold medal turn into a national crusade. To do it in front of the world, to beat the Americans (who, after the World Cup, had replaced the Russians as our great rival), to win the gold medal, to hear "O Canada" played as they raised the red maple leaf to the rafters would be a moment almost as sweet as hearing "Henderson scores for Canada!" The National Hockey League might have been going to Japan to sell T-shirts, but for Canadians, that was merely the smokescreen for a holy mission. Finally, we would get back what was rightfully ours.

And so in the months leading up to the Games of Nagano, several parallel sets of hopes and dreams were in play. The NHL laid the groundwork for a marketing breakthrough, insuring that they received maximum bang for interrupting their sched-ule and taking their show on the road. The Canadian hockey establishment, hoping to rebound from the disappointment of the World Cup, set out to select the management that would in turn select the players who would bring home the gold medal. And the Canadian people fretted, second-guessed, hoped and dared to imagine what it would be like to win an Olympic gold medal in men's hockey.

IN OCTOBER, the National Hockey League took its first ten-tative steps across the Pacific, bringing two teams to Tokyo to open the regular season. Japan had seen this kind of thing before. The National Football League had played exhibition games at the huge domed stadium known as the Egg Dome, filling the place with a crowd more curious than passionate. And of course, touring major league baseball players had made Japan a regular stop over the years, but in those games there was no sense of dislocation – baseball is Japan's pastime as much as it is America's. Hockey, though, was a different matter – pure exotica, a game that hardly registered. The Japanese were more than willing to adopt – and then transform – U.S. pop culture whole hog, but hockey they hadn't yet got around to. If the Olympic tournament were going to be the marketing success the NHL hoped, there was much work to be done.

The two teams chosen to make the trip had obvious strate-gic assets. One, the Vancouver Canucks, hailed from a Pacific Rim city with a large Asian population, a popular vacation destination for Japanese tourists en route to the Rocky Mountains and beyond. Entering the 1997–98 season, the Canucks figured as contenders for a Stanley Cup championship, and they featured two of the game's greatest stars – Pavel Bure, the Russian Rocket, whose skills would surely win over new-comers to the game, and Mark Messier, who had won Cups in Edmonton and New York, being acknowledged along the way as one of the great players, and great leaders, in the history of the game.

Their opponents would be the Mighty Ducks of Anaheim. The Disney connection, the movie connection, the cartoon connection, the Japanese would understand immediately, having embraced that particular bit of Americana, and having their own Disneyland right along the road to Tokyo's Narita Airport. More importantly, the Ducks employed Paul Kariya,

Warm-up act: Mark Messier led the Vancouver Canucks in the NHL's 1997–98 season-opener in Japan, but he would be left off the Canadian team when it returned for the Olympic tournament a few months later.

believed by some to already be the best player in the game. A member of a Japanese-Canadian family – his paternal grand-parents were born in Japan – Kariya would be a huge story the moment he landed in Tokyo. By the time the Olympics rolled around, the Japanese public would have enjoyed endless images of Kariya enjoying the sights and sounds of their country. They would have seen his face on the news, on sports programs, and on the perpetual game shows that are the staple of Japanese prime-time television. He would provide a rooting interest, a cultural link to the sport, a living connection between Canada and Japan. He would sell a whole lot of licensed merchandise.

Or at least he would have had he not been in the midst of a nasty contract squabble with the Mighty Ducks' management. Not yet at the stage of his career where he could declare full free agency and receiving no offers from other teams (who would have had to provide Anaheim with huge compensation had they signed him), Kariya chose to stay home, to refuse to report to the team at training camp. When the Ducks took flight for Japan, he remained at home in British Columbia.

The trip was still a qualified success. The Japanese filled the arena and extended a warm welcome to the players. The NHL marketing arm began to make inroads into one of the largest and wealthiest pools of untapped customers in the world.

But still, the trip could have been taken as an omen, a sign that once the NHL crossed the international date line, nothing would go quite as planned. First, it would be the business of the game, the newfound power of players, that would throw a monkey wrench into the works. A few months later, it would be the glorious, unpredictable nature of the game itself.

WHILE THE NHL was going through its dry run in Tokyo, the process of selecting an Olympic team began under the intense scrutiny of the Canadian public. It should be remembered, in hindsight, that there was little second-guessing over the naming of the team's executive and coach. Everyone agreed that a change was needed after the World Cup, that it was probably time for some of those who had served their country so well in the past – Glen Sather, Scotty Bowman and the rest – to make way for a new generation of leadership. Thus the appointment of Bob Clarke to run the show. The one-time Philadelphia Flyers tough guy, whose most memorable moment in international hockey came when he broke Russian great Valery Kharlamov's ankle with a slash in the 1972 Series, had earned himself a reputation as an astute judge of talent, first in Florida, and then with the Flyers. In the fall of 1997, memories were still fresh of Philadelphia's loss to Detroit in the finals, which, though a four-game sweep, suggested to a lot of people that the NHL's next great team was about to emerge. Working with

As part of the changing of the guard in Canada's international hockey strategists, Marc Crawford was named the coach of the 1998 Olympic team.

Clarke would be Pierre Gauthier, the bright young general manager of the Ottawa Senators, and Bob Gainey, the former Montreal star who had done such a brilliant job building the Dallas Stars into Stanley Cup contenders. Coaching the team would be Marc Crawford, who had led the Colorado Avalanche to the Stanley Cup in 1996.

These would be different eyes than those that selected past Team Canadas, with different loyalties, and a clear mandate to challenge past assumptions. The team they would select would be designed to beat the Americans, to right the wrongs of the World Cup. And if that meant leaving older stars off the squad, if it meant that some who had given long and meritorious service to their country would be denied their one shot at Olympic glory, while others who had been reluctant to play in less glamorous tournaments in the past would be selected, so be it. This was not to be about lifetime achievement awards. This was not about paying back old favours. Unlike the basketball Dream Team, Canada's squad had a tournament to win in which it was anything but a sure thing. Clarke and company knew that they would undoubtedly face some criticism no matter who they chose. If they won the gold medal, no one would care. If they didn't win the gold medal, the blame wouldn't rest with who they'd chosen – it would all come down on their heads.

Obviously there would be some sensitive decisions to make, since several of Canada's greatest players were in the twilight of their careers – and some of them had certainly looked it in the World Cup. One choice was made for them – Mario Lemieux had retired at the end of the 1996–97 season and had made it clear that he would not reconsider his decision, even for the chance to play at the Olympics. Although there had been suggestions that Wayne Gretzky might be a liability, he had shown enough life in the past year with the New York Rangers that there was no way the greatest player in the history of the game would be left off the squad. Paul Coffey, on the other hand, arguably second only to Bobby Orr as the greatest offensive defenceman ever, had clearly lost something. Though his skating skills had been a huge asset when previous Canadian teams played on the large international ice surface, this time he wouldn't be invited along. The next generation, the Rob Blakes and Chris Prongers, would have to fill his skates, along with veteran Raymond Bourque, who had offended some by declining to play for Canada in the past. No place for hard feelings, for settling old scores, with a gold medal to be won.

Clarke and company completed the roster, trying to match stars with role players, to achieve the necessary balance of skill and grit, to put together a team that could become a true team in just a few days together, and not just an aggregation of individual talents. The goaltender? Patrick Roy, always at his best when the most was on the line, would be number one – barring a disaster. The captain? How could Clarke opt for anyone other than his own captain in Philadelphia, the player who would have to dominate during these Olympics if Canada was going to win, the player who would have to dominate two months after the Games during the Stanley Cup playoffs if the Flyers were going to capture a championship: Eric Lindros.

And if Lindros was indeed the captain, what would happen to Mark Messier? Now there was a tough one. The former Oiler, former Ranger, and now Vancouver Canuck, had been the heart and soul of every team he'd ever played for. Any dressing room he entered immediately became his. Leadership had been a large part of successful Team Canadas, going right back to Phil Esposito's role in 1972. Could Canada win without someone like Messier? Could Messier find a place on a team that was supposed to belong to Lindros? And more importantly, was he still good enough to play in this company? During the past season with the New York Rangers, Messier had at times looked like a spent force, and during the World Cup, he had been unable to lift his game to the heights Canadian fans had come to expect.

Messier would not make the decision easy. Any time he was asked, he made it clear that he hoped to be chosen. And those, like Gretzky, who had won championships at his side, also made it clear they wanted him along on the trip to Japan. Didn't he deserve the chance, considering what he'd given to Canadian hockey in the past? Didn't he deserve the chance to have a gold medal hung around his neck? Clarke, Gainey, Gauthier and Crawford understood that they'd have questions to answer no matter what they decided.

On the night of November 29 at the Corel Centre in Ottawa, home of the Senators, Team Canada was unveiled to an anxious, expectant nation. There had been all kinds of informed speculation in the days leading up to the announcement, but no one, not the press, not the players, knew for certain who would be

The crying game: Theoren Fleury celebrated with his wife as he learned he had been named to the 1998 Canadian Olympic team.

named to the squad. In a novel, dramatic twist, the players – who were still engaged in the business of the NHL regular season – would not be introduced in person. Instead, young hockey players wearing jerseys with each team member's name on the back would skate under a spotlight in the darkened arena, taking their place in a line at centre ice.

Theoren Fleury of the Calgary Flames watched on television from his living room, with his wife, his son and his father among those by his side. Most speculative versions of the roster circulated by those in the know had included his name. But still, he wouldn't know for sure that he was headed for the Olympics until a kid wearing a jersey with his name written across the shoulders skated onto the Corel Centre ice.

"I just heard it! I just heard it!" Fleury yelled, hearing his name. Then he fell into the embrace of his family.

There was a kid dressed as Rob Zamuner, the relatively unheralded forward from the Tampa Bay Lighting. And another dressed as Keith Primeau, who toiled in relative obscurity with

the Carolina Hurricanes, who had underachieved with his previous employers, the Detroit Red Wings, but who had represented Canada well during the past year's world championships.
And of course there was a Gretzky, a Kariya, a Lindros, a
Brendan Shanahan, a Raymond Bourque, an Al MacInnis, and
the rest of the players most would have expected to find on a
Canadian Olympic team.

There was no kid wearing number 11, with "Messier" stitched
across the back. There was no last-minute change of heart.
There would be no sentimental gestures.

The torch had officially been passed, and Clarke and
company knew they'd have to explain why. At the press
conference immediately following the announcement, the
Messier/Lindros question naturally came first.

"It wasn't our point to exclude anyone," Clarke said, playing
the diplomat. "We tried to put together what we felt would be
the best team, looking at all the needs of a team. . . . I don't think
it was done because we wanted to change what hockey has been
doing in Canada. But I thought it was time that a new group of
players from our country started taking some responsibility.
Lindros could be the captain for the next Olympics, and the
one after that."

Of course no one would argue with his rationale, no one
would question Lindros's selection or Messier's absence, or any
of the other choices made by those in charge of Canada's team.
Just bring home a gold medal, and the controversy would be
long forgotten.

⁃ᴗ

THE ALL-STAR GAME, held in Vancouver on January 18,
offered a further preview of the NHL's marketing strategy as the
Olympics approached. For the first time, rather than having

The lineup of the 1998 Canadian Olympic team encouraged the usual second-guessing about selections: a Zamuner, but no Messier?

conference face conference – a terrible format that killed any rooting interest for the fans and encouraged the players to simply go through the motions – the league decided to tug at the same nationalist instincts that the Olympics exploits so successfully. The best players in the NHL were divided into two teams, one made up of North American–born players, one made up of everyone else. To read it as Us versus Them wasn't a stretch and was also the perfect prelude to a big international tournament. But it would have taken a seer to spot the most significant bit of foreshadowing. In the penalty-shot contest, held the night before the game, Dominik Hasek of the Buffalo Sabres, a Czech representing the Rest of the World, stopped six of Canada's best in succession, one on one.

ON FEBRUARY 1, in a game between the Anaheim Mighty Ducks and the Chicago Blackhawks, Paul Kariya cruised to the front of the Chicago net and did what he does as well as anyone in hockey, accepting a pass and firing home a goal. At that instant, even as he began to raise his arms in celebration, he was viciously crosschecked across the mouth by Chicago defenceman Gary Suter. Suter just happened to be the same guy whose crosscheck from behind had put Wayne Gretzky out of the 1991 Canada Cup. And he also just happened to be a member of the team representing the United States in the coming Olympics. For many Canadians, none of that seemed like a coincidence.

Kariya's head snapped back. He fell to the ice, eventually rising to his knees, and then was helped to the Anaheim dressing room. He did not return to action that night. The early news wasn't so bad. It was reported that Kariya had suffered a grade one or grade two concussion – the less serious end of the spectrum. He'd miss a game or two, waiting for the post-concussion symptoms to clear up, but it was expected he'd be ready in plenty of time to hook up with Team Canada and head for Japan. Once again, a goodly portion of the NHL's marketing scheme relied on his presence at the Olympics, not to mention the fact that the team desperately needed his scoring skills. "We need him if we're going to win the gold medal," defenceman Rob Blake said. "It would be a devastating loss if we have to play without him."

But Kariya didn't get better. The symptoms didn't abate. The cobwebs didn't clear. The official word remained that he'd be ready. "Deep down, I believe I'll be ready to go," Kariya said. Only on the day the players boarded the plane in Vancouver for Tokyo was it confirmed that Kariya wouldn't be coming along – at least not initially. A roster spot would be held open for a few days just in case he recovered in time to participate in the medal round of the tournament. Meanwhile, the Montreal Canadiens' Mark Recchi, waiting out the Olympic hiatus at his parents' home in Phoenix, was told to get ready just in case he was needed.

He would be, because Kariya wouldn't be coming. He wouldn't play a game for Canada, and he wouldn't play a game for the Mighty Ducks during the remainder of the NHL regular season. In a year in which a concussion ended the career of Brett Lindros, nearly ended the career of Pat Lafontaine, and later caused Eric Lindros to endure a frightening couple of weeks after the Olympics, Kariya's loss was a particularly devastating blow, to the league and to his country. National Hockey League vice-president Brian Burke, whose job includes the less-than-enviable task of doling out discipline, handed Suter just a four-game suspension, based on the fact that Kariya's injury hadn't seemed that serious when it first occurred. Canadian hockey fans were understandably outraged.

In Japan to watch the tournament, Burke knew what people were saying back home, and he knew what Bob Clarke, the former ankle breaker, was saying right there – that there was no way Suter should be allowed to participate in the Olympics. "Four games is ridiculous for what he did," Clarke said. "He could have ended this kid's career, and the league doesn't help [Kariya]. . . . This guy almost kills Paul Kariya, and he only gets four games." Burke heard all of that, and he knew that his countrymen thought it was a crime that Suter could be here representing his country after preventing Kariya from repre-senting his.

"Even if I'd given Suter more games, it wouldn't have affected this," Burke told Canadian Hockey's Bob Nicholson in a con-versation in Nagano. "Even if I'd given him 20 games, he'd still be playing [here]. I don't know why everyone is mouthing off about it."

They were mouthing off about fair play, about justice, about a gold medal that they wanted so, so badly. No cheap shot in a game that meant next to nothing should be able to take that away.

·ᴖ

THE DAY THE Canadian team arrived in Nagano, the ruling powers of hockey held a press conference in the temporary media room erected next door to the Big Hat Arena, the main venue for Olympic hockey. The rink would have looked odd to anyone familiar with the North American version of the game. Though apparently NHL-sized when viewed from the outside, inside it seated only 9,000 fans, enough to provide a nice home for a major junior franchise in Canada. The stands seemed temporary – as indeed they were, since the moment the Games were over, the Big Hat would be converted into a convention and trade centre. It's not as if hordes of Naganoites would suddenly be desperate for ice time after the Olympics. The sport remained obscure to the locals, to the point that during the tournament, at least half the seats were filled by the relatively few foreign visitors – North Americans and Europeans – who had made the long trip to Japan, along with athletes from other sports, the press and a large section (often three-quarters empty) reserved for International Olympic Committee members and other officials. While they cheered for hard body checks and eventually began to appreciate passing and goal scoring, the biggest cheers from the locals were reserved for the beginning of each period, when a specially commissioned Olympic pop song repeated the refrain "Face Off! Face Off!" over and over.

So no, the great Japanese hockey revolution had not yet taken place (though the national teams in both the men's and women's tournaments naturally received the same passionate support as all of the other Japanese athletes in the games). Still, sitting at a table in the front of the room, NHL commissioner Gary Bettman, National Hockey League Players' Association president Bob Goodenow, and Rene Fasel, the head of the International Ice Hockey Federation (the "amateur" governing body that for so long was Canada's nemesis), seemed extremely pleased with what they saw.

"We are together now in the family," Fasel said, enjoying a moment of triumph in which he had played the tiniest of parts.

The turnout of reporters from every country represented at the Games was proof enough that hockey had become the marquee sport of these Olympics. To that extent, the great experiment of shutting down the NHL at mid-season had already borne fruit. Hockey – and presumably very good hockey – was going to receive exposure in places where it had previously been ignored, even if Canadians at home would have to rise at dawn to get their fill because of the time difference.

"The Olympics has become the best of best in all sports," Bettman said. "For many years, there were some hockey professionals playing for some countries and not for others. Here, people are going to see hockey at its highest level, see the best players in the world representing their countries. I suppose that's what the Olympics are all about."

Of course, there is also a danger in saying something like that if you are the president of a professional sports organization whose bread and butter is not a once-every-four-years Olympic tournament, but the 82-game regular season and playoffs. Understanding that, Bettman, while willing to celebrate the Olympic experience, also took pains to protect his primary product.

"As excited as we are to be here, and how exciting we expect the tournament to be," he said, "what still motivates our players is the NHL season and the Stanley Cup."

It motivates them because that's what they are paid to do,

and because the Cup still retains its mystical hold over hockey players, because having your name engraved on it still holds tremendous meaning, because playing the game for money is still far more than a job for the vast majority of those who do it.

But if one competition could challenge the quest for Lord Stanley's Cup (and could easily surpass the largely meaningless NHL regular season), it was the opportunity to win an Olympic gold medal. For the players born in Europe and in the former Soviet Union, the Olympic Games (and to a lesser extent, the world championships) had always been held out as a national goal, and those who had won them were acclaimed as heroes. For the North American players, a few of whom had played in the world championship, a handful of whom had participated on previous Olympic teams, this was a once-in-a-career opportunity.

This was bigger than just a hockey tournament, even the greatest hockey tournament anyone could imagine. This carried with it as much history, as much tradition, as any single sport championship. This was the Olympic Games, this was for your country, this was the flag being raised and the anthem being played, this was being presented with a medal that not even the most inflated athlete's salary could buy. This, for every player, from every team, was the Big One, the Biggest One. For this, for a gold medal, they would give their hearts.

But for each of the contending teams in the Olympic tournament, the stakes were just a little bit different.

The Americans, icing essentially the same side that won the World Cup, came to Nagano as co-favourites to win the gold medal. Player for player, they had already proved themselves Canada's match, and their coach, Ron Wilson, had shown himself capable of turning a group of all-stars into a cohesive unit. The only question would be about goaltending. Mike Richter of the New York Rangers had been brilliant in the

World Cup and was the single biggest reason for the Americans' upset victory. But during the NHL regular season, he hadn't been his dominating self. For the United States to have a chance, Richter would have to find a way to regain his form.

If both Canada and the United States stumbled, surely Sweden would be ready to claim the gold. They had won it in 1994, and the star of that tournament, Peter Forsberg of the Colorado Avalanche, was back to lead the team along with Mats Sundin, a brilliant player whose talents were largely wasted with the inept Toronto Maple Leafs. The Swedes' chances diminished somewhat when Ulf Samuelsson was ruled ineligible for the tournament because he had taken out U.S. citizenship. Still, the team seemed certain to reach at least the semi-finals.

Next in line were the Russians, a pale shadow of the former Big Red Machine of the Soviet Union, but still a side with enormous offensive talent. Goaltending was a huge question mark, since Nikolai Khabibulin had declined the invitation to participate – an example of the acrimony and politics that has been so much a part of Russian hockey since the breakup of the Soviet Empire. Neither was anyone sure how Sergei Fedorov would fit in. A restricted free agent who had turned down all offers from the team with which he had won the Stanley Cup the previous season, the Detroit Red Wings, Fedorov had spent most of the fall and winter following his teenaged tennis player girlfriend, Anna Kournikova, around the women's professional circuit. He had decided to use the Olympics to get in shape and to showcase his skills for potential bidders. If his teammates accepted him, if the Russians could get along, if Pavel Bure could play up to the level of his skills, if coach Vladimir Iourzinov could keep the various factions at peace and keep order without resorting to the iron-handed tactics of Viktor Tikhonov, then the Russians would have to be taken seriously.

NHL contract holdout Sergei Fedorov (centre, chatting with former goaltending great Vladislav Tretiak) led a Russian team that was hard to evaluate.

There were also the Finns, who had occasionally excelled in top-level international tournaments and who could boast Teemu Selanne and Saku Koivu, two players who could be found on any list of the best in the world. On occasions, they had risen to the challenge internationally when least expected.

No one talked much about the Czechs, except for Jaromir Jagr, and especially Dominik Hasek. The season before, Hasek had been recognized as the most valuable player in the National Hockey League, in addition to winning the Vezina Trophy as the league's best goaltender. Hasek played his position as no one had before. His style could be found in no textbook – flopping, lurching, sometimes dropping his stick and grabbing the puck with his blocker hand, sometimes flipping the puck in the air and whacking it down the ice with his stick, baseball style. The goaltending coach of the Buffalo Sabres, Mitch Korn, could show with diagrams and vectors how Hasek covered more ice and more of the open net than any other goaltender in the NHL. But watching him, it seemed both spontaneous and undeniably brilliant. He alone had turned the sad-sack Sabres into a playoff team.

And then during those playoffs the previous spring, in a game against the Ottawa Senators, he had left the ice with a mysterious injury, never to return. He had decided that he didn't like coach Ted Nolan, who would be fired at season's end despite the great season. He attempted to choke a Buffalo reporter who suggested in print that he'd faked his injury and quit on the team. He arrive at training camp the next fall to find out that one of his own teammates, Matthew Barnaby, had threatened to run him for the role he'd taken in Nolan's forced exit.

Hasek, if he was on, could beat anybody, anytime, all by himself, sage hockey folks whispered before the Olympic competition began. If Jagr, the sometimes petulant superstar of the Pittsburgh Penguins, could be persuaded to play his best hockey, he might score enough goals to give the Czechs a chance. But looking at a roster that included only a handful of players who could be considered regular NHLers, and eight who hadn't played a minute in the league, it was tough to make the case that the Czechs could stand up to such formidable opposition.

But in all of those pre-tournament assessments, one factor about the Czechs was invariably overlooked. During the World Cup, they had been terrible, failing to advance beyond the preliminary round in Europe. It was obvious to those involved with the team that the problem had been largely emotional, that the Czech NHL stars had never meshed with those who had been playing back home, that the clash of egos and temperaments had poisoned the dressing room. For all its talent and despite the fact that, on paper, it should have been a medal contender, the Czech team had simply imploded.

This time, they would do things differently. The bulk of the squad would be assembled not from NHL stars, but from lesser players competing in Europe. That would surely have a beneficial effect on team chemistry. And that would also produce a squad familiar with playing on the larger European ice surfaces – the same sized ice they'd see in Japan. It's not an enormous difference between NHL rinks and international ice surfaces, but it can be tremendously important to the way the game is played, changing the angles of attack and defence. None of the Canadians and Americans would have experienced the big ice recently, and some wouldn't have experienced it at all. But the Czechs, with the exception of a small core of NHLers, including Jagr and Hasek, would face no adjustment whatsoever.

By the time they handed out the medals, that factor would prove rather significant.

·⤳

THE PRELIMINARY ROUND of the Olympic tournament, featuring the teams hoping to qualify for the medal round, certainly wasn't going to change the face of the game. A hockey historian might find it intriguing to watch the former Soviet republic of Kazakhstan, playing like a museum replica of the 1970s' Big Red Machine, but otherwise this was familiar, Grade B international hockey. Free flowing on the big ice, but without the intense physical play of the NHL, it wouldn't have turned the heads of most Canadian hockey fans.

But from the beginning of the real tournament, when the United States met the Swedes in the opening match of the second round, that perception changed entirely. Because of the NHL-friendly format, the big teams were playing only for pride and seeding in their opening games. Still, even without much at stake, this was jaw-droppingly brilliant hockey, of a calibre and kind never seen before. This hybrid game, combining the best players in the world on the large ice, competing passionately for their countries, was better than the World Cup or the Canada Cup (played in North American rinks), better than anything during the NHL regular season, better than all but the most dramatic moments of the Stanley Cup playoffs. It was hockey the way we all imagined it was when we were young, up and down the ice, free of clutching and grabbing, five, six, seven, even eight minutes between whistles. No fighting, no pointless scrums, no commercial time-outs, speed and skill coming to the fore, the best players being allowed to show their best. During the rare stops in play, those in the arena who understood what they were seeing were left shaking their heads, taking deep breaths and muttering "Wow."

The Swedes won that first game 4–2, the first hint that the Americans might not be quite the powerhouse everyone had expected. Team Canada made its debut later against a lesser foe, Belarus, another former Soviet republic that was one of the qualifiers. It was a one-sided affair, as could have been expected, but still the NHL stars seemed a bit anxious at times. During his early shifts, Lindros appeared to be trying to flatten anyone with a pulse who happened to be wearing the opponent's sweater. And Gretzky, far more a play-maker than a scorer in the latter stages of his career, fired shots from all angles and all places on the ice. He had scored so many goals, so many goals that mattered, and yet one in the Olympic Games would obviously mean so much.

After the 5–0 win, Canada moved on to a game against Sweden in which the value of Patrick Roy was proved beyond any doubt. In the past, Roy had been passed over for international assignments, including the World Cup, in part because of a long-running feud with Edmonton general manager Glen Sather, who assembled many of Canada's teams. For the Olympics, he was handed the number one job by his Colorado coach Crawford and told that he'd start every game in Japan barring injury (Curtis Joseph and Martin Brodeur would serve as a rather capable pair of backups). He'd earned that nod by being the ultimate "money" goaltender. In a game with nothing on the line, he could look ordinary. But give him something to play for, and he could be better than anyone, as he proved winning two Stanley Cups for the Montreal Canadiens, and another for the Avalanche. There could be no greater occasion than the Olympic Games, and so Roy figured to be brilliant. Against Sweden, he put on a show, his tremendous skill and even more tremendous confidence stymieing a very good offensive team again and again. Canada won the game 3–2 and, given the way the Swedes had handled the Americans, looked very much like the class of the field.

Only one preliminary round game remained: a World Cup rematch against the United States. The last game between the two countries, in the fall of 1996, will be remembered as a humbling moment for Canadian hockey and the dawn of a new world order, with the Yanks replacing the Russians as our primary rivals. This game would simply be for bragging rights, a scene-setter for the showdown that would surely follow, perhaps in the gold medal game. Still, given recent history and given that it would be the first real test for this version of Team Canada, there was plenty of tension, plenty of atmosphere, as team captains Eric Lindros and Jeremy Roenick prepared to take the opening face-off.

"Now listen to me," referee Bill McCreary said to them before dropping the puck. "We're going to have a really good game and there's gonna be no bullshit. You play like men and you're going to get treated like men."

There were no physical fireworks, just plenty of exciting, passionate hockey. Again, Roy's goaltending was the difference, just as Mike Richter's work had made the difference for the United States in the World Cup. The Canadians' 4–1 win over the Americans meant that Canada would advance undefeated to the quarter-finals, drawing the lowest ranked team on the other side of the draw – qualifier Kazakhstan. During the world junior

If Canada or the U.S. stumbled, surely Sweden, the 1994 gold medalists, would take the gold. But the Swedes, defeated 3–2 by Canada in round-robin play, failed to make the medal round.

tournament a few weeks before, Canada had lost to Kazakhstan's national junior team, an event viewed with some alarm by the folks back home. There was no such problem in Nagano – Team Canada, playing with tremendous confidence, dispatched them easily, winning 4–1, and outshooting their opponents 37–17. With the victory, Canada moved on to the semi-finals, one win from a guaranteed medal, two wins from gold.

The way the draw had played out, it seemed likely Canada would be facing the United States again in the semi-finals. But the Americans, who had never really found their focus in Japan, fell instead to the Czech Republic, and especially to Hasek, 4–1. Gone was the new nemesis, the World Cup champion: the path to the gold medal suddenly seemed much simpler. Beat the Czechs, beat the winner of the game between the Russians and the Finns (who had upset Sweden), and claim the Olympic championship.

BECAUSE OF THE WAY the game ended, because so much
has been written and said about its final moments, what went
before has already been largely forgotten: The Czechs' com-
plete dominance in the first period, when Team Canada seemed
lost on the big ice and were beaten to every loose puck; more of
the same in the second period, still with no score; the goal that
put the Czechs ahead early in the third, a slapshot by Jiri Slegr
that slipped past Patrick Roy on the stick side; the realization
with 10 minutes left in regulation that Canada was losing, that
they deserved to be losing, that the Czechs seemed every inch
the better team despite the all-star pedigree of their opposition.

What Canadians would choose to remember are the final
minutes of the third period, when their heroes suddenly came
to life, as if they finally understood what was on the line.
Outplayed and outsmarted throughout, they took over the game
as though it were purely an act of will, pushing the Czechs back
into their own zone, forcing Hasek to make stop after stop. And
then, with a little over a minute left, came the goal, Trevor
Linden banging in a centring pass from Lindros to tie the score.
The Canadian bench erupted in celebration. The Czechs, as
though beaten rather than tied, slumped to the ice.

If Canada had gone on to win, if they had converted any of
the many chances that they enjoyed in overtime, then Linden's
goal would have been remembered along all of the great ones,
from Henderson on down. The victory, in a game in which they
were badly outplayed for most of three periods, would have been
romanticized, turned into another example of Canadian pluck,
heart, grit – how even with their backs to the wall, Our Boys
find a way to get it done. And if they had done that, if they
had beaten the Czechs, would they have also beaten the
Russians for the gold medal? Perhaps. Probably. A coming-of-

age moment for Eric Lindros. The perfect career-capper for Gretzky. Confirmation that Marc Crawford was the best coach in hockey, that Bob Clarke knew what he was doing when he shook up the Canadian roster. Proof positive that, all things being equal, the game is ours, and was ours, and would have been ours all those years when our best players weren't welcome at the Olympics.

Instead, with his teammates falling back around him in overtime, Hasek turned back just about everything, and Canada simply missed other opportunities. At the end of the extra frame, the Czechs seemed ready to celebrate and the Canadians were deflated, because both understood what would come next: a shootout, a penalty-shot contest, a chance for Hasek to win the game all by himself.

"It's big pressure for a goaltender," Hasek said. "I like the pressure. You make a great save, and even maybe if you don't have such a good team as Canada or Russia, you can beat them."

⸱⸜

ANYONE WITH EVEN a passing knowledge of the sport agrees that a shootout is a lousy, unfair way to decide a hockey game of consequence. "It's an artificial contest," says Ken Dryden. "It's a contest that bears no relation to the rest of the game." It would be like settling a basketball game with a free-throw–shooting showdown, settling a football game with a passing drill. Better to play on, however long, until the game is settled with a goal. But in international hockey, it doesn't work like that, and everyone including Canada knew that going in.

That said, there was no evidence that the brain trust of Team Canada had spent an inordinate amount of time considering the possibility. After the completion of overtime, the coaches were asked for a list of the five players on their team who would participate in the shootout. It's the kind of decision that ought to be made ahead of time, and not in the heat of the moment. But though there may have been conversations at some point between Crawford, Clarke and the rest as to who would take the shots, by all appearances the list was drawn up then and there on the bench. In the days and weeks and months that followed, those choices were debated even more hotly than the Olympic team selections. Crawford's picks, in the order they would shoot: Theoren Fleury. Raymond Bourque. Joe Nieuwendyk. Eric Lindros. Brendan Shanahan.

No Wayne Gretzky, the greatest scorer in the history of the game (but to be fair, never known for his success on break-aways). No Steve Yzerman. Joe Sakic, if he hadn't been hurt, would surely have been there. Paul Kariya, if he'd been able to make the trip to Japan, surely would have had one of the five spots. Raymond Bourque? The ice had been chewed up and wouldn't be resurfaced after the overtime, Crawford explained later. Pure shooters would have an advantage over those trying to finesse a goaltender out of position. Bourque, in all-star game skills contests, had shown himself to be the most accurate shooter in the sport. "I think he's been proved through the years to be great on breakaways," Crawford said afterwards, though none of the hockey people around could summon up memories of the defenceman breaking in on his own.

But maybe against Hasek, in that place, at that time, maybe it wouldn't have mattered who took the puck. Maybe he just couldn't have been beaten. Maybe, once Robert Reichel fired the puck just inside the post and past Patrick Roy on the Czech's first shot, it was all over anyway.

As each Canadian shooter missed, the tension in the arena, and on the bench, grew nearly unbearable. "I knew that the ice was bad, and it would be difficult to deke," Fleury said. "I made up my mind right away to shoot." Hasek stoned him, and then

Bourque, and then Nieuwendyk. Lindros would come closest – trying to go high, he clipped the crossbar with his shot. Because Roy had been brilliant as well, stopping all but Reichel's shot, Brendan Shanahan skated to centre ice with a chance to keep Canada in the game. But he seemed hesitant from the moment he took the puck, unwilling to just let fly with a shot, unsure what move to make. Finally, he made a half-hearted shift to his right and tried to slip the puck under Hasek's pads. It was not close, not close at all.

"You let your country down," Shanahan said afterwards. "You let your teammates down. It's a completely empty feeling. You just want to stick your head in the ground."

Hasek dropped to his knees and kissed the ice, as his teammates piled on top of him in celebration. "We played like a team," Jaromir Jagr said later of the greatest moment in Czech hockey history. "We never played like that before. We played good defence, tried not to make mistakes, scored some goals and hoped that Dominik would stop all the shots."

The Canadian players skated onto the ice for the post-game ceremonies, clearly in a state of shock. "It was almost like someone close, like a family member, had died," Fleury said. High in the stands, Bob Clarke sat with Gainey and Gauthier, staring straight ahead, expressionless, his head in his hands.

For the longest time, Wayne Gretzky sat alone on the Canadian bench, gazing into space, understanding that his first and last and only chance to win an Olympic gold medal was over. He would finish the tournament with four assists, without a goal, without the career-capping moment he so clearly desired.

"Whether you're a seven-year-old playing a tournament game or a 37-year-old playing in a game like this, it's devastating," he would say later. "You never get over it. You're never ready to accept it. Each and every time it's very difficult to accept and understand. . . .

Written off as medal contenders, the Czech Republic took advantage of Dominik Hasek's extraordinary goaltending to oust Canada in the semi-finals.

"You always want to be able to say our country is great. But by losing, I don't think that our hockey is being destroyed in Canada. People love our game. They love our sport. They want us to win every game. Every time you put on a Canadian uniform and play for Team Canada, anything but gold is not acceptable. And that's a pressure and a fact of hockey that our team lives with, that maybe no other team has. When you win, the roses are tremendous. And when you lose, you've got to stand up and take your lumps. We're taking our lumps."

⁙

THE OTHER BAD NEWS of the day would take second place, at least in Canada, at least for a while. A few minutes before the game between Canada and the Czechs, Gary Bettman emerged from a television interview in a studio beneath the stands to find himself surrounded by reporters in search of answers. They had learned earlier in the day that members of the United States team, after losing to the Czechs and thereby losing their chance at a medal, had returned to the Athletes' Village after a night on the town and caused considerable damage, smashing chairs and setting off fire extinguishers. It later became clear that this was only the wildest of several raucous evenings the American hockey players spent in Nagano and that other U.S. athletes had complained about their behaviour, about how they'd made so much noise that those with competitions the next morning had been unable to sleep. One member of the U.S. cross-country ski team later recalled how drunken hockey players had stumbled into his room in the middle of the night, believing it was theirs.

Perhaps in other circumstances, it would have been forgiven as the kind of boys-will-be-boys antics that one might expect of young men on the road. But this was different. This was Japan, where etiquette and protocol are all, where it's serious business to deviate from accepted norms. And this wasn't just another hockey tournament, but the Olympic Games. Until that moment, the professional hockey players had seemed to have been acting like model Olympians, far more than the basketball Dream Teams ever did. They'd stayed with the other athletes, slept in the same relatively spartan quarters. Hockey players – especially members of the Canadian team – became a familiar sight at other events, cheering on their countrymen.

The incident in the Village sent absolutely the opposite message – that these spoiled pros didn't belong here, that they didn't respect the Games, their hosts, the whole idea of the Olympics. They had thumbed their noses at all of it and then, without fessing up, without apologizing, they'd caught the first plane back to North America, having no interest in seeing the competition out or in participating in the closing ceremonies.

Rambunctious American hockey players, some captured on tape whooping it up late at night in Nagano during the tournament, gave the NHL's Olympic venture an ugly black eye.

For the great NHL experiment, nothing, not even the failure of the Canadian and U.S. teams to advance to the gold medal round, could be worse, given the way the news played in North America. Even in corners of the United States where hockey claimed little space in the public imagination, the notion of ignorant, room-wrecking drunks struck a nerve.

But in Japan, Bettman, as savvy as he is, didn't seem to understand that or to anticipate the repercussions that followed. For someone with such a finely tuned sense of image management and sensitive to the ways of the press, he was several beats slow with his reaction. While he said the NHL was taking the incident seriously, that it was investigating, that it would surely get to the heart of the matter, everything about his manner and his choice of words suggested otherwise. "It was less than $1,000 worth of damage. It's not like some dormitories were completely destroyed," he maintained, mentioning that he'd just had lunch with International Olympic Committee president Juan Antonio Samaranch, who he said was equally unconcerned. Clearly, Bettman hoped, and expected, that the incident would simply blow over and be forgotten, that in the wake of the wonderful hockey being played in the tournament, surely no one would remember such a minor incident. And surely they wouldn't feel that this was a sign that big-money professional athletes didn't appreciate their chance to take part. "I think that's an unfair generalization," Bettman said. "Remember, there were people who didn't even think that our players would stay in the village – and they did. . . . It's grossly unfair to suggest that this represents anything to the Olympics other than the actions of a couple of guys."

As to what the league planned to do about the players' behaviour, the commissioner tried his best to sound tough. "I have broad powers under the NHL constitution to discipline players for conduct detrimental to the league. How you choose to define it and apply it, we'll leave for another day. I don't want to speculate."

The NHL would do nothing. Despite much private speculation, the guilty players have never been identified – the U.S. team closed ranks, and whatever investigation the NHL carried out might as well been orchestrated by Inspector Clouseau. Chris Chelios, who was apparently not one of the room-wreckers, eventually offered a donation to pay for the damage. The United States Olympic Committee threatened to bar every member of the 1998 team from participating in the 2002 Games in Salt Lake City.

And all across the United States, in the hockey-mad regions and in all of those places where the NHL still hopes to sell the game, the incident hung on like a bad smell. It hadn't been a great Games for the Yanks in any case. Even Canada had finished ahead of them in the medal standings. Taped television coverage designed to overcome the time difference had only served to bleed events of any drama.

Ask an American what he or she remembers about the Winter Olympic Games in Nagano and what would the answer be? Tara Lipinski, Nancy Kwan, and a bunch of drunken big-money professional hockey players who obviously shouldn't have been invited in the first place. To think they shut down the NHL season for that.

·⤳

ON THE LAST DAY of the Games, the Czechs won the gold medal, defeating the Russian team 1–0, thanks in large part to Hasek's brilliance. It seemed as though the entire population of the Czech Republic had risen at dawn to watch the game shown live on television, and as the final seconds ticked down, they moved into the streets to celebrate. More than 70,000 packed Old Town Square in Prague, wrapping the statue of St. Wenceslas in the Czech flag. After the game, the players, including those who would soon return to their NHL careers, made the long trek to Prague, where they were greeted as conquering heroes. Václav Havel, who noted all of the Hasek For President signs, offered to swap jobs with the goaltender.

There were no such celebrations in Canada. The day before, against a Finnish team without its best player, Teemu Selanne, who had been forced out of the line-up with an injury, and featuring an unknown goaltender named Ari Sulander, Team Canada had fallen 3–2 in the bronze medal game. After the tremendous emotional intensity of the semi-final against the Czechs, the Canadians seemed drained and played half-heartedly. Roy seemed especially affected by the circumstances. Perhaps Crawford ought to have known that without a gold medal on the line, his goaltender would lose his edge. Perhaps

More than 70,000 packed Old Town Square in Prague to welcome home Dominik Hasek and the rest of the Czech team, the unlikely victors in the 1998 Olympic tournament.

he ought to have given Joseph or Brodeur the start. But this had been Roy's tournament from the beginning, and his play certainly wasn't the reason that Canada had faltered. Unfortunately, his play had quite a bit to do with Canada's loss to the Finns when he gave up a couple of very suspect goals that his teammates were unable to overcome.

And so there was no medal. Nothing. After all that build-up, all that anticipation, all those dreams, Canada, the hockey nation, was left asking one question: What the hell happened?

·

THE ANSWER BECAME apparent following a period of anger and mourning and reflection and healing.

What happened was that Canada lost, fair and square. The United States lost. Sweden lost. By any measure, all but the distracted Americans could just as easily have won the gold medal. The tournament was that close, the other teams were that good.

The National Hockey League lost. Aside from re-awakening the passions of hockey fans in the Czech Republic, and perhaps sowing a few seeds in Japan, the great marketing gamble had been a failure. Kariya wasn't there. The marquee teams didn't make the final. Some of the American players disgraced themselves. The only consolation came from the fact that the games took place when most of North America was safely tucked in bed, and that there were four years left to work out the bugs before Olympic hockey went prime time in Salt Lake City in 2002.

The Czechs won, obviously. The Russians won, with so much working against them. The Finns won, beating their Swedish arch rivals and capturing a medal.

And the game won. Hockey won. It proved to be beyond being choreographed, beyond being scripted. It proved that in its purest form, it was close to perfect, so fast, so thrilling, so unpredictable. The repercussions from the tournament would be felt immediately after the players returned to their regular jobs in North America, as the NHL altered its rules and its officiating, trying to make its everyday product look just a little bit more like the magical, glorious sport that had been on exhibit in Japan.

· OUR GAME ·

ON JUNE 5, 1997, just as the Detroit Red Wings were closing in on the Stanley Cup, Peter Pocklington spoke the words long dreaded by hockey fans in Edmonton, Alberta, and across Canada: The Oilers were for sale, for real. No more crying wolf. No more empty threats. Winnipeg was gone. Quebec City was gone. Another domino was set to tumble.

For the better part of a decade – since not long after he peddled Wayne Gretzky to the Los Angeles Kings in August 1988, forever earning the fans' enmity – Pocklington had been alternately poor-mouthing and bullying the city. Unless they agreed to various concessions, the Oilers would leave town.

In April of 1993, he had threatened to move the franchise (a franchise he'd bought in 1976 with Nelson Skalbania from Dr. Charles Allard when it was part of the World Hockey Association – payment had been a Renoir painting, his wife's 12-carat diamond ring, a million dollars out of their pockets and a million dollars that they borrowed) to Hamilton if his demands for a better lease agreement at Northlands Coliseum weren't met. By September of that year, he was asking for permission from the National Hockey League to shift the Oilers to Minneapolis. That had been stopped by an injunction, but three years later, Edmontonians were told by the league that if they didn't buy 13,000 season's tickets, the team's future was in peril. They anted up.

No, Pocklington they wouldn't miss, even though he had

The Edmonton Oilers were the last great dynasty of the modern NHL, with five Stanley Cup wins from 1983–84 to 1989–90. But Edmonton's status as the smallest market in an expanding league began threatening its very survival.

controlled the Oilers through their glory years in the 1980s, when Gretzky, Mark Messier and the rest were winning a string of five Stanley Cups in seven seasons and redefining the game in their own exciting image. The owner's deteriorating personal finances, his enormous debt to the Alberta Treasury Branches combined with the ever-increasing costs of operating an NHL team had long ago killed the magic and turned the Oilers into one of the league's poor sisters.

Pocklington had sold Gretzky and he had allowed Messier to leave for the New York Rangers, where he would win another Cup. With Pocklington's personal financial problems and the team's relatively tiny payroll, Edmonton would need enormous good fortune to compete for a championship ever again. And so those who loved the Oilers would have been thrilled to see Pocklington go, would have celebrated his

On June 5, 1997, Peter Pocklington made the announcement Edmonton fans had long dreaded: The Oilers were for sale – for real.

announcement, but for one small detail: who other than Peter Puck would be crazy enough to want to operate a franchise in the league's smallest market?

"I've done my best to keep the team here in the past, and I will do my best to sell the team to people who will keep it here in the future," Pocklington said. "Our first priority is to seek local investors to step forward and take my place."

Those sentiments sounded both familiar and hollow to Canadian hockey fans, who already felt their hold on the national game slowly slipping away. In 1995 and 1996, the Quebec Nordiques and Winnipeg Jets, unable to convince local or provincial governments to build them new arenas and subsidize their operating losses, packed up and left for the United States. In Quebec, there seemed little will to save the team, even though it was an exciting, competitive club that would win the Stanley Cup during its first year as the Colorado Avalanche. In Winnipeg, though, the Jets' exit had been prolonged, emotional and, finally, heartbreaking. A local ownership group was cobbled together to buy the team from Barry Shenkrow. Children

Despite fervent support among some fans, in 1996 the Winnipeg Jets went the way of the Quebec Nordiques, relocating to an American city.

smashed their piggy banks to contribute a few extra dollars to the cause. A great public rally was held to show just how much the team meant to the city. But in the end, the dollars simply weren't there, the city was simply too small – too small, at least, to support a franchise in the modern NHL.

Those taking the long view could argue that the departed teams (along with the Hartford Whalers, who would move on to Carolina) were historical anomalies in the first place, the remains of the World Hockey Association absorbed by the NHL as part of the deal to eliminate a competitor. Under normal circumstances, the NHL would never have awarded teams to cities of that size, and as the league grew and payrolls increased, their demise was inevitable, no matter how anyone felt. Their failure was an unfortunate by-product of the league's success, of its evolution into big-time North American sport. Winnipeg and Quebec didn't belong in a league with New York, Los Angeles, Chicago, Toronto and Montreal. The great unguarded border between Canada and the United States was all but meaningless in the restricted free market of professional sport. Eventually,

the teams would go where the money was, where the population was, where the dollars coming in were worth the same
as the dollars being paid out in salaries.

Of course there was a cultural argument as well, one lost not
just on the new American owners, but seemingly on the custo-
dians of the game, on the people who operated the NHL's head
office in New York, and in particular on the man at the top,
commissioner Gary Bettman. These weren't just businesses
fleeing south for a better deal. These weren't just entertainment
options being lost, like a restaurant or a movie theatre that had
suddenly shut its doors. Sure, life would go on without them,
the money spent on tickets would be spent elsewhere, local
economies wouldn't really suffer.

But how to measure the loss that wouldn't show up on any
bottom line, the blow to civic identity, the detachment from the
rest of Canada, the rest of the continent? And how to convince
Canadians that what they considered their game, their invention, their property, wasn't rapidly being consumed by the great
colossus to the south? Defining Canada had always been a tricky
business for Canadians but for two unassailable truths – that the
national culture wasn't American, and that hockey was a part
of it, in every province and territory.

Now the Avalanche would move and immediately win the
Stanley Cup for a city that had no idea what that trophy really
meant. Now the Winnipeg Jets – the team for which Bobby Hull
had toiled, that had played beneath a huge picture of Queen
Elizabeth in its arena, the team that had made many a long,
tough prairie winter that much more tolerable – had become
something called the Phoenix Coyotes, playing hockey in a
place where snow and ice and the Queen and the Trans-Canada
Highway and Anders Hedberg were as exotic as the North Pole.

That might be logical and economically sound, it might
satisfy market forces, but to Canadians it just wasn't right.

Neither was it right that the Edmonton Oilers, a great and storied franchise, a dynasty just a decade ago, was about to be parcelled off to some place like Texas. They might have heard of Gretzky in Houston, but they certainly wouldn't understand what he meant, they wouldn't know what it was to watch him parked behind the opposition goal, controlling the entire game by himself, flipping a soft pass to a place where a teammate would materialize to fire it into the net. They wouldn't have any shared memory of dawn rides to the local rink, of home-town heroes who played their way through the ranks to the best league in the world, of Saturday nights in front of the television, of Paul Henderson's goal. That was ours and ours alone, and surely you couldn't put a price tag on it.

They had done just that, though. The day that Pocklington held his press conference, optimism about the state of Canadian hockey was at a low ebb. There had been eight Canadian franchises in the National Hockey League. There were now six. Soon, there would be five. Then four. Then three. Toronto, Montreal and Vancouver certainly weren't in peril, each a city with enough size and enough corporate wealth to support a team no matter what the league's future. Still, didn't somebody care that the sport was abandoning its roots, giving up on the one place where it really mattered? How had it been hijacked?

There were other dramatic stories that would hover over the games of the 1997–98 season, from the Red Wings' long-awaited Stanley Cup triumph to the Olympics in Nagano to the fall of Alan Eagleson. But none said more about the state of the game in the last years of the century, none better reflected the conflict between the business of hockey and the game's place in Canadian culture, than the battle to save the Edmonton Oilers.

It really began in the fall, just as the season got underway, and was not completely resolved until spring, when the playoffs were already well underway. There was a happy ending, but it was a false coda: the costs of operating a team continued to rise, the Canadian dollar continued to tumble, the economics of doing business in Edmonton, Calgary and Ottawa made less and less sense. This little drama seemed destined to be repeated, and the conflict between hockey the business and hockey the national institution seemed to be just beginning.

·‿

THE ECONOMICS OF the Oilers' sale were simple enough to understand. The National Hockey League had just completed an expansion process that would add four teams to the league (none of them in Canada, of course), for which new owners in Atlanta, Minneapolis, Nashville and Columbus were willing to pay through the nose. The going price for an NHL team had been established at $85 million – U.S. No team with players and with a farm system that was put on the block could possibly be worth less. The other owners each had a vested interest in that new bottom line.

The Oilers, operating in Edmonton, certainly weren't worth $85 million, based on their costs and revenues. The most recent estimate by *Financial World* magazine, which annually rates the value of all teams in the major professional sports, had tagged the Oilers' value at $50 million. Take that same franchise, though, and move it somewhere else, and the price would rise accordingly, which was of considerable interest not just to Pocklington, but to his major creditor, the Alberta Treasury Branches. By virtue of monies borrowed to keep the Oilers and Northlands Coliseum in business, and just as significantly to pay off debts left behind by the failed Gainers meat-processing empire and other less-than-successful entrepreneurial schemes, Pocklington owed the ATB an awful lot of money – in excess of

$100 million. Though he said that he was selling the Oilers so he could commit more time to rest and relaxation, the truth was that he had no choice in the matter, that he was being forced to sell in order to pay off those onerous debts. It followed, therefore, that while he might be willing to pay lip service to the notion of finding local ownership, his real interest was in getting as much money for the club as possible, which would almost certainly mean selling to U.S.-based interests.

According to Pocklington, the culprits (aside from his own business failings) were player salaries and the economic structure of the league, which didn't include large-scale revenue sharing among franchises. "By our first and second Stanley Cups, and even our third and fourth, the total team salaries were about $6 million Canadian," he said. "And then, unfortunately, all hell broke loose. By 1990, our salaries had gone to an extreme of $8 million or $9 million Canadian. This year they will be $30 million Canadian, perhaps $40 million Canadian. Unfortunately, the price of entertainment, the players' salaries, have exploded in the face of revenues that have maybe doubled."

Blaming players for escalating player salaries – as fans often do when the latest multimillion-dollar contract is announced – misses the point entirely. For decades, salaries in the NHL remained artificially low because the players were, first, without any union and then without an effective union to represent their interests. While other athletes in other sports fought successfully for free agency and a greater slice of team profits, most notably in baseball, hockey players fell farther and farther behind. That began to change in the 1980s and into the 1990s. Players won limited free agency and survived a management lockout designed to impose a salary cap.

Though the best players still weren't able to sell their services on the open market during the peak years of their careers, free agency became a reality for those in their early thirties. The team owners were more than happy to enter into bidding wars, pushing salaries skyward of their own free will. The problem was that the tremendous disparity in revenues between franchises made a level playing field impossible. Clubs with huge local broadcast contracts or operated by mammoth corporations would always have a tremendous advantage over those like the Oilers, operated by one wealthy – but not Disney-wealthy or Gulf-and-Western wealthy – individual.

That system wasn't about to change. The NHL wasn't about to enter into the kind of full revenue sharing found in the National Football League that enabled a small market team like the Green Bay Packers to thrive. "To hell with the small markets," New Jersey owner John McMullen had said during the 1994–95 lockout. His comment seemed to sum up the attitude of the U.S.-based owners. The problems in Edmonton and elsewhere weren't their concern, at least as long as there were other U.S. cities willing to take any team that might want to move.

Pocklington and his creditors understood that and also understood that long-term survival in Edmonton was looking less and less likely. His first rescue plan had been to take 45 per cent of the team public, selling shares to raise cash and cover his loans, but the stock offering wouldn't materialize in time to keep the ATB at bay. He was left with no choice but to sell everything to settle his debts – and if an Edmonton-based individual or group came along, that would be just fine. But since they'd face exactly the same daunting economic challenges he'd faced, since Edmonton isn't chock-a-block with billionaires, the far more likely possibility was that an American would scoop the team up and move it elsewhere.

Only one complication stood in the way of that scenario. In 1994, following his last showdown with the City of Edmonton over control of Northlands Coliseum, Pocklington had made a few concessions of his own. In return for a better arena deal, he had pledged to keep the Oilers in Edmonton until 2004. Not only that, but he had agreed that if he ever decided to sell the team, local investors would be able to purchase it for $70 million, even if a higher offer was on the table from outside interests. Should a local group fail to materialize, and should Pocklington accept an offer from an outside buyer, the city would have 30 days to find someone (or a consortium of several someones) willing to buy the team and keep it in Edmonton.

The summer and the first weeks of the autumn of 1997 were filled with rumours about potential buyers, about local interests trying to put together a bid. One day it would seem that the Oilers were surely gone, the next that a local saviour would be unveiled at any moment. But no locals came forward with anything resembling a concrete offer. With the blessing of the ATB – or more correctly, with the ATB forcing his hand – Pocklington followed through with what had seemed inevitable from the start, selling the team to a U.S. buyer.

On February 10, 1998, after circling around the team for several months, Leslie Alexander, the owner of the Houston Rockets of the National Basketball Association, officially offered Pocklington $82.5 million for the Oilers, an offer that he accepted, and more importantly, that the ATB accepted. Alexander pledged to keep the team in Edmonton for three more years. If it was losing money at that point, he'd either be given an NHL expansion team, or he'd be allowed to move the Oilers wherever he chose. The clock was ticking for the city. Thirty days to go.

⋅◞

THOUGH THE WHOLE RANGE of problems faced by the Oilers are unique to Canadian franchises in the National Hockey League, they certainly aren't faced by every team on this side of the border. Within Canada, there is a class system that mirrors the class system of the NHL as a whole, a gulf between the haves and have-nots nearly as large as that between the Oilers and the New York Rangers. Though the Canadian teams would eventually go together in front of a federal government committee to plead their case, as though they were all in the same boat, the Oilers, Flames and Senators came from an entirely different universe than the Toronto Maple Leafs, the Montreal Canadiens and the Vancouver Canucks.

Consider the kind of questions each team faced on a daily basis. In Calgary, though the team draws well and though there is a healthy corporate sector to fill the private boxes and the club seats, the basic issue of money in, money out remains a daily concern. All of the available revenue streams (ticket sales, sponsorship, broadcast rights) can't compare with what teams in larger cities can attract. The Flames maintain the lowest payroll in the National Hockey League. The more dollars the team can earn, the more it can pay players, and the better chance it has of winning. There is no individual among the club's seven-person ownership consortium who can go out on a limb, spending (and losing) millions of his own dollars in order to attract a big-name free agent or to get into a bidding war for one of the club's home-grown stars.

"I would love to stay in Calgary for sure," the Flames star forward Theo Fleury said, understanding that his contract was about to run out. "But hockey is a business now, and Calgary's a small market team, and there's only so much they can pay and afford to pay."

Ron Bremner, the broadcast executive who is the president and CEO of the Flames, explains how each ticket sold counts. "If we take in $4,000 a night for a suite, times 40 games, that's $160,000, times two that's $320,000 – that's the left leg of a third-line forward. Now what we have to do is find opportunities

Franchise star Theo Fleury works out with his Calgary teammates. "I would love to stay," he said.

to get the right leg. Then we start working on the torso. That's what you have to do. You have to break it down. As somebody once said, How do you eat an elephant? One bite at a time. That's what we're doing here. We're eating elephants every day."

The Toronto Maple Leafs fly in a private chartered jet to their away games. The Vancouver Canucks have gone one step farther, purchasing their own airplane to make travel even more convenient. The Edmonton Oilers, with the most remote and least convenient locale in the entire league, fly commercial. Bill Tuele, their vice-president of public relations, checks the team in at the airport counter, worries about late arrivals, makes sure that if the team is stuck with middle seats, they're doled off to the rookies. Like Bremner, he understands that the inconvenience that goes with such economies hurts the team over the course of a long season – but that it's also part of a larger equation that makes it possible to remain in business.

Rod Bremner, president and CEO *of the Flames, explains how to pay for a third-line forward, one leg at a time.*

"If a decision has to be made between $2 million to go towards a player or operating the team as opposed to flying on a charter plane, then that decision is fairly easy to make. The team that charters has at least a five-to-ten-point leg up on everybody that doesn't. . . . Is it better to sign another player, or to give in to a player to keep him in Edmonton, or to charter? It's just a grim reality of economics. You only have so much money coming in."

The Ottawa Senators are in a slightly different category. As their former general manager, Pierre Gauthier, pointed out (bucking the party line in the process), Ottawa shouldn't really be considered a small market, at least in the context of professional hockey.

"People talk about the small market. That is such a fallacy in terms of Ottawa. There's a million and a half people within a 50-mile radius, and it's a white-collar town. There's high disposable income here, as high as there is anywhere in Canada. And everybody's a hockey fan. You go to places like Dallas,

Phoenix, St. Louis. In places like that, the population is larger, but who's a hockey fan? And there are so many other sports that they compete with. Here, we're the only game in town."

But the Senators have been behind the eight ball since their expansion birth. The original ownership, banking on real estate developments around the Corel Centre in suburban Kanata that never came to pass, paid a then astounding $50 million for the team – just as the league demanded – even though at the time the figure didn't really make sense. They started life playing in a converted junior hockey rink, with just 10,000 seats, before moving into a beautiful new $230-million building that they paid for themselves. By then, though, the team had established itself as the league's laughing stock, abysmally managed, utterly inept even by expansion standards. The seats were priced to pay the bills, but the product on the ice was distinctly minor league – and so fans, even in a hockey town, were reluctant to turn up. It wasn't until a thrilling run to the playoffs in the 1996–97 season that Ottawa was finally fully won over by the hockey team built by Gauthier and coached by Jacques Martin.

For all three of the have-not franchises, cash was and would continue to be an issue, especially in a league in which player salaries would increase (as they have increased in all professional sports), and in which revenues were only partly shared.

The richer clubs would claim that they, too, had to be concerned about red ink. In fact, though, their situations were vastly different. The Vancouver Canucks, owned by the wealthy American John McCaw, and part of the larger Orca Bay sports/entertainment empire that also included the Vancouver Grizzlies of the National Basketball Association, could afford to maintain one of the league's higher payrolls and compete for the services of the most expensive free agents. There were operating losses, but those McCaw happily covered out of his own pocket.

The Montreal Canadiens, corporately owned in a large city where hockey is religion, would suffer somewhat from economic ups and downs. But it was always with the understanding that their market included not just the city of Montreal, or the Province of Quebec, but a national audience raised on "Hockey Night in Canada" and enraptured by a long string of Stanley Cups that extended nearly to the present. In 1997–98, they made the biggest profit of all the Canadian teams.

Toronto is a special case. The Maple Leafs had not won a championship since 1967, and for most of the intervening years had been a franchise caught somewhere between mediocre and terrible. But that had nothing at all to do with money. Conn Smythe had made a fortune after building in the depths of the Depression an arena that came to be known as the Carlton Street Cashbox – tickets at Maple Leaf Gardens, no matter the price, no matter how bad the product on the ice, were always sold. Harold Ballard's own idiosyncrasies were the main reason the team didn't succeed during his long tenure. But from shareholders, there were few complaints.

The Leafs sat smack dab in the middle of Canada's most populated region and its largest media market, meaning that their local radio and television rights were by far the most valuable in the country. Like the Habs, they enjoyed a national following, thanks to their dominance of Saturday nights for so many decades. And demand for seats and for private boxes always far exceeded the supply – so much so, that season's ticket holders were loath to give up their place. For corporations, being able to give a valued client a good pair of tickets to a Leaf game was the best possible reward. No matter how much the business of the National Hockey League might change, the basic truth of the hockey business in Toronto would remain the same: owning the team was a licence to print money.

In 1997–98, while the Oilers were fighting for their very

survival in Edmonton, while the Flames and Senators confronted serious cash shortages, the Maple Leaf ownership had very different concerns. The first was having the club shifted to the NHL's Atlantic Conference, a pet issue of the Leafs' new president, former Montreal goaltending great Ken Dryden. There, the great rivalry with the Canadiens – reduced to two games a year under the NHL's existing alignment – could be re-ignited, in theory bringing back some of the magic, playing to the fans' nostalgia for a simpler, six-team hockey universe.

A lovely idea, even if it was hardly crucial to the Maple Leafs' well-being (whether it was the Habs or the Carolina Hurricanes in town, all of the tickets would still be sold). But it was not such a lovely idea for Toronto's country cousins in Edmonton and Calgary. For the Flames and Oilers, the Leafs' regular season visits represented sure sell-outs, more evidence of the team's national fan base. If the Leafs shifted conferences, there would be only one visit a year, a change that teams flying coach and keeping track of every roll of tape could hardly afford. "It's a nationalistic issue," Calgary general manager Al Coates explained. "It's not just money. It keeps Canada whole, the rivalries going."

When the National Hockey League governors convened in the first week of December 1997 for their annual meetings at The Breakers, a luxurious resort in West Palm Beach, Florida, the potential Leaf move was near the top of the agenda – not that every team was equally interested. "The only ones that care are the Canadian teams," said Tampa Bay president Phil Esposito, once upon a time of Sault Ste. Marie, Ontario, once upon a time the man who led Team Canada to its emotional victory over the Big Red Machine of the Soviet Union in the first Summit Series. "The rest of us don't care. I don't care where they go. It doesn't matter to us."

Dryden made an impassioned, eloquent speech to the governors and, more importantly, commissioner Gary Bettman

Calgary general manager Al Coates reflected on the consequence of fewer home games against Toronto, if the Leafs succeeded in switching divisions, seeing it as "a nationalistic issue."

brokered a compromise that would allow the Leafs to shift conferences, but guarantee extra Toronto games to the western Canadian teams. The motion passed with just two abstentions and was hailed as Dryden's first triumph as team president.

"The challenge of any league that has a lot of teams is to build some familiarity and intimacy in it," Dryden told a crowd of reporters afterwards. "It's not very interesting to play an opponent that nobody knows very well. Now you've got that greater sense of closeness and attachment that is both physical by distance and psychological by history and practical in terms of number of games."

The Maple Leafs' other principal concern was the location, design and construction of a new arena to replace venerable Maple Leaf Gardens. The last of the Original Six rinks still in its original form, the Gardens is a charming antique, a museum

At the NHL governors' meeting in December 1997, Phil Esposito (left), general manager of the Tampa Bay Lightning, told his Edmonton counterpart, Glen Sather (right), that when it comes to the divisional aspirations of Canadian NHL teams, "I don't care where they go."

of hockey history, but also inadequate for the revenue requirements of a big-time, big-league franchise. The Leafs needed more luxury box space, they needed club seats, they needed better concessions, all with the idea of squeezing still more dollars out of the Toronto market. Dryden envisioned a new hockey shrine to replace the old one, something equally monumental.

Steve Stavro, the grocery magnate who controlled the franchise, seemed more concerned with the hard numbers. During a fact-finding tour of Washington's new MCI Center, Stavro – who rarely utters a word in public – was full of questions about the most expensive seats in the house. "You've got 7,000 below the boxes, closing right around the bowl. Do you call these anything special? Platinum seats or anything?"

Remember that precious metal.

Various plans were floated for a new Maple Leaf Gardens, all of which ignored the fact that one of Toronto's other big-league teams – the Raptors of the National Basketball Association –

In February 1998, the Toronto Maple Leafs bought the National Basketball Association's Raptors and took over construction of their new facility, modifying the Air Canada Centre for hockey.

was already far along in the construction of a new arena of its own, the Air Canada Centre. It wasn't good enough, it wasn't grand enough, it wasn't in the right location, Stavro and company said over and over. And then, in February 1998, in one of the largest transactions in the history of Canadian sport, the Leafs bought both the Raptors and the building from their previous owner, Alan Slaight, and the new building was just fine. Maple Leaf Gardens' remaining lifespan as an NHL rink was shortened from a few more years to a few more months. The Leafs' management hurriedly drew up plans to redesign the inside of the Air Canada Centre to suit their needs and especially to give a posher look to the public spaces, befitting a legendary franchise.

Then came the payoff. In June 1998, the Leafs announced that their season's ticket holders, already paying the highest prices in Canada to watch professional hockey, would be the first in the NHL forced to cough up an additional "licence" fee. It meant paying for the right to buy tickets in the building's most expensive section. Those sitting in the 1,500 seats closest to ice level would be charged $15,000 per seat up front, an annual (there it is) "Platinum Club" membership of $2,500, plus $115 per ticket per game on the sides, a mere $110 on the ends.

The average ticket price, which had been less than $35 in the Gardens, would jump to $76.44 at the Air Canada Centre. Ticket revenues for each game would be $1.4 million – twice what they were in the old building. "If you want to golf at the Rosedale Golf Club, you've got to pay Rosedale prices," the Leafs' alternate governor Brian Bellmore explained, comparing the team to the city's poshest neighbourhood.

If the Leafs were the Rosedale Golf Club, Edmonton, Calgary and Ottawa were the pay-as-you-play public links. While they could certainly use the money, their market would never bear such an audacious cash grab as licence fees. But in Toronto – and the Leafs knew it better than anyone – there would be grumbling, but in the end the price would be paid.

THE MICHAEL LARGUE AFFAIR was a tragi-comic subplot to the main drama of the Oilers sale in Edmonton. The self-proclaimed New York investment banker, who had relatives in the city, rolled into town early in 1998 and announced his intention to buy the hockey team and keep it in Edmonton. It wasn't the first time he'd surfaced in NHL circles, having previously made inquiries about the Tampa Bay Lightning and the Hartford Whalers. Largue claimed that his backer, a mysterious Swiss businessman named Lester Mittendorf, was willing to spend $100 million to buy the team and keep it in Edmonton.

He claimed that his own background included playing hockey on a U.S. college scholarship as well as with a Swiss pro team. He explained that Mittendorf was the owner of a club called the Bern Bears and had a passionate interest in the sport.

It certainly sounded too good to be true, but still, initially, Largue won the confidence of many in Edmonton, including some members of the local press who should have known better. But gradually, with even minimal investigation, his story began to unravel. His academic record was exaggerated, and in places entirely phony. There was no record of his hockey career. No one by the name of Mittendorf was associated with hockey in Switzerland, and in fact there was no record of anyone named Lester Mittendorf anywhere. Largue maintained that his mystery man was real, even as it was revealed that there were more skeletons in his closet – that he had been convicted of grand larceny for stealing money from the co-op apartment where he lived, that he has been suspended by the U.S. securities industry for unauthorized trading. Largue was a charmer, and he was represented by a high-powered, well-known lawyer, an association that bought him a little bit of credibility. But in the end, after a few whirlwind days when he was the subject of every headline, Largue was revealed as a phony and disappeared as quickly as he had appeared, never to return.

IN THE END, the Largue fiasco only served to provide a damaging distraction from the process of finding a legitimate local buyer in Edmonton. Once he was gone, the pitch to potential investors resumed, directed as much to the heart as to the head. As a place to sock away a couple of million dollars, there were certainly all kinds of less risky, more attractive options, and those with a gambling bent would have been better advised to head for a Las Vegas roulette table and pick themselves a number. A creative thinker could come up with a scenario under which the Oilers might break even, or at least minimize their operating losses from year to year. But no one was going to get rich becoming part of any consortium that would buy the team from Peter Pocklington. Not in 1998, not in Edmonton, not in the current National Hockey League.

But sports ownership, even for the richest of the rich, has always been about more than the bottom line. It's not the potential for annual profit that lures buyers to professional franchises, especially in an era when the price of those franchises is escalating beyond all reason. There might be the odd tax advantage involved, there might be the possibility of cashing in at a later date, selling the team when the going rate for a franchise has become even higher. The real kick, though, comes from buying something that's more fun than an office building, sexier than junk bonds, more high profile than a widget factory. Own a team and you get the best toy imaginable, you become a player, you get your name in the newspapers just as often as you'd like, and if you have other high-profile businesses, perhaps they'll be enhanced by your association with something the public so obviously appreciates. Ego, fun, community service: those three factors, in that order, explain virtually all non-corporate sports ownership.

No one in Edmonton was wealthy enough (or at least wealthy enough and willing) to assume the position of sole, or even majority owner, and so all of those factors would have to be subdivided several ways. No one would be able to put his own stamp and name on the team the way Pocklington had. It would be fun to be associated with an NHL team, but that fun would be mitigated by fear – of mounting losses, of where the league's costs were headed, and (for the truly far-thinking) of a pending collusion suit by former players which, if successful, could wind up costing each franchise several million dollars as part of a set-tlement. With the Oilers, the best selling point would at the same time be the most square: doing something for the city in which you live, spending money to enhance the quality of life for others, to give everyone a little emotional boost. Putting money into the Oilers would be about Edmonton as much as it would be about hockey, and those who invested would have to believe, with their hearts and their wallets, that it was worth the risk to keep the team in place.

After some initial confusion, the full financial proposition began to take shape. The NHL would allow a potential owner-ship group to borrow half of the $70 million (U.S.) franchise cost but no more. It wasn't just a matter of Gary Bettman being tough on a Canadian small market: a team loaded down by debt would have little chance of long-term survival. Beyond the cost of the franchise, the new owners would have to show that they had $5 million in operating capital. A team too cash-poor to do business once the owners had paid for it wouldn't be of any use to anyone.

The original core of partners came together rather quickly and included most of those who would be considered Edmonton's movers and shakers: Ed Bean, whose other high-profile foray into professional sport had been underwriting a pro-posed fight between Mike Tyson and Razor Ruddock at Northlands Coliseum, which had fallen through when Tyson developed a mysterious illness; Cathy Roozen, heiress to the Allard family fortune; software entrepreneur Bruce Saville; Jim Hole of Hole Engineering, who had once served as president of the Edmonton Eskimos of the CFL; and car dealer Ron Hodgson. The *Edmonton Journal* bought in, as did five businessmen from Lloydminster, as did Cal Nichols, the lawyer who took the lead role in putting the consortium together. Eventually, there were 35 members in all, including a later arrival, comic book artist

Edmonton lawyer Cal Nichols worked the phones, assembling a last-minute consortium of local investors to keep the Oilers franchise in town.

Todd McFarlane, the creator of Spawn and a native of Calgary. Each investor contributed a minimum of $1 million. None contributed more than $5 million.

"What we tried to do was sell it on the basis of community-first motives, as opposed to for profit," Nichols said. "I like to think of the group that we've brought together as the blue-collar millionaires of the market. Many of them are people who have worked hard, got down in the trenches, rolled up their sleeves and have been successful in manufacturing and distribution and in some of the oil field supply companies. There's not anybody in this group who are junk bond dealers or a lot of major corporations. These are real grass-roots millionaires that are participating in this project."

Together, the original core of investors brought about $25 million to the table, $10 million short of the necessary total. But after that, there seemed to be a dearth of people who felt the call of community service – at least at that price – and so the pickings became exceptionally slim. For Nichols and the others involved in trying to raise the money by the deadline, their task became one of soliciting, cajoling, pressuring, pleading, begging – it was more like a telethon to cure some terrible disease than the assembling of investors.

"Our chances of finding a bunch of people with $100,000 to get us the ten million that we need in the next two days – I don't like our chances of that," said Doug McFarlane, one of those working with Nichols to drum up potential partners. "And we don't want people going out and breaking their piggy banks and borrowing money to do that, because we can't guarantee the return."

It wasn't just wealthy individuals who were reluctant to jump on board the Oilers bandwagon. Many of Edmonton's most significant corporations, most notably the large oil companies that were so important to the province, were reluctant to come forward with sponsorship dollars. Alberta premier Ralph Klein sent letters to all of the right people, and Nichols hoped that political pressure might be effective, since so many of the companies were at the mercy of provincial regulation.

Still, the rejection letters piled up in Nichols's office. Even a scheme to rename the Oilers' arena Petroleum Place and decorate it with the names and logos of the province's biggest oil and gas companies was rejected across the board. If big companies didn't want to be part of an Oilers resurgence, what would that say to other potential investors, who might be still sitting on the fence?

"The equity guys in this deal that are putting their own money up have to look at this and say, I'm going to risk my money and find that the biggest corporations in Alberta aren't interested in commercial support," said Reg Barry, another of those working with Nichols. "That's got to send up a red flag.

You've got to say, you know what, maybe this isn't the right place for an NHL hockey team."

Forty-eight hours before the deadline, the final $10 million had yet to materialize. Twenty-four hours before the deadline, and still they were short the necessary cash. The night of the twelfth, the wee hours of the thirteenth, the members of the consortium met, hoping for a last-minute windfall, prepared to decide whether the Oilers could be saved.

"If this issue was a Toronto issue, if the Toronto Maple Leafs were leaving Toronto under the same kind of conditions and economic duress, I'll tell you that they'd be lining up on Bay Street at King to say what can we do to help," Barry said. "We've got to fight and scratch and say, geez, we're out here 2,000 miles away, but we also have five Stanley Cup banners up here and a heritage and a legacy, and we need your help. And so far it ain't working. So there is only one group of guys that are going to make this call, and that's the guys that are going to be sitting around tonight until all hours and looking at each other and saying, Are we going to go or not? And if we're going, boy, we're taking some huge risks."

⁓

DENNIS MILLS HAS a knack for getting his name in the news, especially considering that he's never been given a prominent role in the governing federal Liberal Party. The member for Toronto's Broadview-Greenwood riding is considered a bit of a renegade within caucus – so much so that at one point he actually quit to sit as an independent after his friend, MP John Nunziata, was expelled by the party. What Mills lacks in real clout, he more than makes up for in media savvy, especially when it comes to sports, an area most politicians avoid unless a photo opportunity with a championship winning team is involved. Perhaps it's because his son, Craig, was a top junior prospect, perhaps it's because of his ownership and management role with the St. Michael's Majors of the Ontario Hockey League. Whatever the case, if there is political hay to be made from sports, Mills is normally in the forefront. He was one of the prime movers behind a government committee that briefly threatened to intervene in the 1994–95 NHL lockout. And most notably, he became the chairman of the parliamentary subcommittee investigating professional sport, whose mandate was to take an extremely broad look at the business of sport in Canada.

While the shift of the Winnipeg and Quebec City franchises to the United States lay at the root of the committee's origins, by the time it came together to begin hearings, the questions it was considering stretched beyond hockey to all of the pro sports in Canada. Representatives of the country's two National Basketball Association franchises, its two major league baseball teams, as well as of the Canadian Football League all took their turns explaining the challenges they faced staying afloat in the 1990s – though there was really no legitimate point of comparison among them.

All of that was window-dressing. Everyone understood that the real showpiece, the real main event of the hearings, would be the appearance of the Canadian NHL team owners, along with NHL commissioner Gary Bettman. Hockey, more than any of the other games with the exception of football, could claim cultural and historic significance on the Canadian landscape. And given the fact that two teams had already left, and that others were apparently in peril, these witnesses would be in the strongest position to make a case for some form of government assistance.

Two weeks before his trip to Parliament Hill, Bettman gave a clue as to the nature of that pitch when he made a speech to

Toronto MP Dennis Mills (left) convened a parliamentary subcommittee on professional sport in 1998, attracting the participation of NHL commissioner Gary Bettman (right), who argued for tax breaks for Canadian NHL teams.

members of the Canadian Club in Toronto. It seemed an obvious trial balloon, a way of testing the tolerance of the public for what would surely be perceived as handouts to rich team owners.

Bettman chose an interesting tack. Rather than simply trying to scare the fans and their elected representatives with the threat that more teams might leave, he attempted to build a rational, dispassionate, by-the-numbers argument. Teams based in the United States, he said, had an advantage from day one, based on various government schemes to lure them to cities, an overall lower tax rate, and of course the fact that their revenues were in U.S. dollars. How could a Canadian franchise compete with a team in the States that had been given a government-built arena, that could exist without paying municipal taxes, that sold tickets in the same currency that it used to pay salaries? By contrast, consider the Ottawa Senators, who were forced to pay for a highway overpass to service their arena in Kanata. (Bettman didn't bother to point out, of course, that it was the

Senators' choice to build in the middle of nowhere, part of Bruce Firestone's great real estate scheme that failed.) Look at the Montreal Canadiens, he said, who built their own new arena in downtown Montreal with their own money, and yet had to pay municipal taxes on the property (municipal taxes like other businesses pay, and municipal taxes that they must have understood were in place before putting a shovel in the ground, but be that as it may . . .).

It's your choice, Bettman said, treading a fine line so as not to appear to be an Ugly American telling Canadians how to run their country. But look at Winnipeg, look at Quebec City. You understand the consequences.

The second half of Bettman's argument was anchored in much shakier ground. He attempted to make the case that NHL franchises were significant enough as businesses, as employers, as economic engines, that they ought to be granted the kind of concessions that might be made if a large manufacturing concern moved into town. The commissioner attributed what seemed like a staggering and unlikely number of jobs to each of the Canadian teams and suggested that, without them, their home communities would be significantly the poorer, not just in a psychological or emotional sense, but in cold, hard cash.

Under scrutiny, that argument held very little water. Thanks to some of the outrageous government handouts offered to lure or keep pro sports franchises in the United States, a significant body of economic literature had been produced, evaluating subsidized stadium construction, tax breaks for teams, and the real economic impact of even the largest sports franchises on a community. The conclusions in virtually all of the scholarly papers and books were strikingly similar: sports franchises were small business, not big business; rather than creating economic activity, they actually sucked it out of other parts of the economy, usually other parts that created more jobs for more people;

pouring tens of millions of dollars into arena or stadium construction was rarely a wise investment by government, except as a way of revitalizing the neighbourhood in immediate proximity to the facility, usually at the expense of other neighbourhoods; when team owners cried poor, they were almost invariably lying.

In the NHL, in Canada, you could certainly argue the last point, at least with regard to the smaller markets. The Winnipeg and Quebec City moves suggested that hockey owners weren't crying wolf as much as those in other sports in other places had in the past. Still, if you were going to try to argue that the loss of the Jets had been a significant one for the city, hard economics wasn't the best way to go, especially given the huge amounts of government money the team devoured during its final seasons in Manitoba.

Bettman received a rough ride in the Canadian press after his speech, and the whole notion of tax breaks for hockey teams seemed to raise the hackles of those Canadians who were not as wildly in love with the game as so many of their fellow citizens. But the commissioner, a bright, canny fellow, understood his audience. It wasn't the reporters that he needed to impress, or those who weren't hockey mad in the first place. He wanted to strike a chord with the hard-core fans, to give them a logical base to justify their feelings. And especially, he wanted to give the politicians a way to justify a handout. Emotionally, culturally, saving Canadian hockey teams was a motherhood issue. Add some kind of economic argument to go with it, even if it was voodoo economics, and surely it would carry the day in Parliament.

On April 28, representatives of the Canadian franchises in the National Hockey League teams made the trip to Ottawa to formally make their case. They were received with almost embarrassing enthusiasm by the committee members, especially

Dryden, who as a former superstar player was treated with something approaching reverence.

"There were really only two points we were trying to make," Bettman explained afterwards. "The first is that NHL hockey is an important business and economic engine. There are 11,000 jobs that are attributable to NHL hockey and the arenas [in Canada]. There's a billion dollars of private money that was invested in infrastructure improvement to Canadian communities. There is $300 million in taxes that our teams pay. And therefore we want some recognition that we're more than just some sport. We're an important business."

Other owners and general managers added details to the argument. Rod Bryden, chairman of the Ottawa Senators, dismissed the notion that if Canadian cities could no longer afford to be part of the NHL, they could simply form their own Canadian league (a suggestion made by Phil Esposito, among others). "It would not be the same. It matters that the New York Rangers are here tonight. It matters that we're part of the best in the world and not just the best in Canada. But if we're going to do that, we're going to have to find some way to have the playing field not so completely uphill that the best players can't be held at the top of the hill and just always run down to where the money is. To do that, one can either find some way to tell the United States that you should legislate something to prevent subsidizing pro sports teams. Good luck. Or we can find some way to impose fewer public burdens on Canadian sports teams."

For Ronald Corey, president of the Montreal Canadiens, taxes were the most important issue. "We gave the three levels of government last year $30 million in different taxes. This includes the GST, the Quebec sales tax, the building tax, the business tax, the capital tax. This is all revenue for the three levels of government, and they don't have to invest one dollar."

*Toronto Maple Leafs president Ken Dryden addressed reporters at the Mills
parliamentary subcommittee hearings. He spoke of a have/have-not world in
professional sport, in which some franchises had "no possibility of winning a
Super Bowl or an NBA championship or a Stanley Cup."*

"The issue is, are our teams being taxed into oblivion?"
Bettman wondered.

It was left to Dryden to strike a note closer to the fans' hearts
– especially since those fans, taxpayers themselves, might not be
automatically sympathetic to wealthy owners complaining about
the GST. What would all of this mean to the product on the ice,
to the home team, to its chances of bringing home the Cup?

"What you can start to see happening in sports is teams that
will never win a World Series; there is no possibility of them
winning a Super Bowl or an NBA championship or a Stanley
Cup," Dryden said. "And you never want to get to that point.
We're not there, but we're treading around the edges in some
cases."

Lost in Dryden's characteristic eloquence was the fact that
what he said wasn't true, at least in one notable example. In the
National Football League, every team has a real chance to win

the championship, including the one based in the smallest market in all of professional sports, the Green Bay Packers, who took the title in 1997.

The reason has nothing to do with tax breaks or government subsidies (though individual NFL teams have certainly used their clout to win concessions and have stadiums built, threatening to move if their demands aren't met). Revenue sharing is the key: if teams share the wealth and have approximately the same amount of money coming in, the playing field tends to level itself. But in the case of the NHL, that would involve a radical restructuring of the way the league does business, a restructuring to which the large market teams would never consent.

It simply doesn't matter to the New York Rangers or the Los Angeles Kings that there is a team in Edmonton (in fact, they'd prefer it in a U.S. city that was easier to reach and more identifiable for U.S. fans). Besides the compensation fund set up to allay the costs of a tumbling Canadian dollar, the other teams wouldn't spend a dollar of their money to ensure Ottawa, Calgary and Edmonton's continued survival.

That fine point, though, seemed lost in the wake of the NHL's slick presentation. Though other committee members would say later that tax breaks for pro sports franchises would be hard to justify until the leagues got their own houses in order, the committee chairman was unreserved in his enthusiasm for what he'd just heard.

"How'd you like our submission?" Bettman asked chairman Mills after it was over.

"I think it was outstanding," Mills said, nearly giggling. "Last week, I said the NBA was the best we'd had. Now I'm forced to say, oh my goodness, this is even better."

• ✎

BY THE TIME Cal Nichols and the members of the Oilers ownership consortium stood before the assembled group of reporters on March 13, 1998, the happy word was already out. They had come up with the money. Faced with losing the franchise, the local corporate community had found the final $10 million, expanding the consortium. Few of the investors could feel comfortable with their decision, understanding the apparently impossible challenge that lay ahead. But still, the Oilers had been saved. They would remain in Edmonton. The challenge had been met. The city had come together and preserved something that it held dear.

In Edmonton, in Alberta, in the West, across Canada, one could sense a huge sigh of relief as Nichols stepped to the podium to make the announcement.

"This is going to be a great day for Edmonton," he said. "As of this afternoon the Edmonton investment group has delivered an offer and the required deposit to purchase the Edmonton Oilers. I want you to know that our group of investors. . . ."

His next words were drowned out by applause.

⌣

THE OILERS HAD NOT followed the path of the Jets or the Nordiques, they hadn't taken a place beside dead franchises like the Hamilton Tigers and the Montreal Maroons in hockey history books, but what did that really mean now and into the future?

In the heady days following the sale to Edmonton investors, the can-do spirit still held sway over the fans and over the new owners. The Oilers were going to qualify for the playoffs. They had a roster packed with bright young talent acquired by Glen Sather. Perhaps in the near future, another championship banner could be added to the five that hung from the rafters at

In the small-market world of the Edmonton Oilers, players fly commercial, not charter, so the team can make payroll.

Northlands Coliseum. Perhaps there could be a second golden era for Edmonton hockey.

"I think the plan is to keep the team here forever," said Barry Weaver, a member of the ownership consortium. "Small market. Make it work in a small market. I think if we can make it work here we can set a real precedent for Canada and Canadian hockey. It's part of our culture and our heritage so let's keep 'er here."

Brave words and noble sentiments, neither of which meant much when applied to the modern business of NHL hockey. The new Oilers' owners promised to push the team's payroll from $18 million to more than $26 million by the next season. But according to Pocklington, they'd been losing significant amounts of money at the lower figure, and already one player in the NHL – Detroit's Sergei Fedorov – had signed a contract that would pay him more than Edmonton was prepared to pay its entire roster for a single season.

When Sather heard the news that the sale had gone through, he was in the middle of a golf game with Pocklington. While saying that he was happy with the fact that the team would stay in Edmonton, he seemed less than optimistic about the franchise's future without a single, deep-pocketed owner to pay the bills.

"If this is a Band-Aid solution, then it's not going to solve a thing," he said. "It's going to surface again in three or four years."

The Oilers' biggest star, goaltender Curtis Joseph, would become eligible for free agency at the end of the season. Sather had declined to trade him away, perhaps aware that he added value to the franchise, perhaps gambling that new owners would be able to pay him enough to keep him with the team. But that seemed unlikely now. "We've got a problem with Curtis Joseph," Sather admitted. "He's a free agent. I've been trying to sign him for a year. If an American team wants Curtis bad enough, they'll pay him whatever he wants." And of course there would be no blank cheques in Edmonton.

Nothing would change fundamentally for the small-market Canadian teams, Sather said, until the NHL secured a major league U.S. network television contract to make up for the operating losses. "We have to have a major television contract to survive. That's going to be the saving grace of the Canadian teams – especially Edmonton, Calgary and Ottawa."

But how likely was that, really? Who would pay that kind of money, especially after Fox's ratings for the 1998 playoffs (well promoted and well produced, whatever Canadian fans felt about the glowing puck) fell far below expectations? If U.S. television didn't ride to the rescue, how would teams like the Oilers, the Flames and the Senators survive into the next century?

"We've got to find a way to keep our game at home," Pocklington said. "What has to happen in my opinion in the NHL – and I might be shot at sunset at the next board meeting for saying something such as this – we've got to share all revenue equally beyond gate. That's the only way we're going to keep our game in Canada."

Canadian fans surely wouldn't appreciate being lectured by the Man Who Sold Gretzky, the Man Who Left the Oilers in the Lurch, any more than the other NHL owners would.

Still, if the business of hockey had any interest in preserving the culture of NHL hockey in Canada outside the country's three largest cities, it would require more than government tax breaks. Restructuring would be a tough sell in a league where the U.S. owners haven't shown any inclination to bend over backwards to help Canadian teams survive. But not as unlikely as finding a group of people in Edmonton, Alberta, to put up $50 million, with only their fondest hopes and wildest dreams as collateral.

⸱⸱

ON JULY 15, 1998, the Toronto Maple Leafs held a press conference to announce the most significant free agent signing in their long history. Curtis Joseph, considered one of the best two or three goaltenders in the NHL, had committed to the Leafs for four years, for a salary of $24 million. He would be expected to help lead the team back to respectability, to be the face of a new era in franchise history as the team moved to the Air Canada Centre. Just as importantly, his presence would make it a little easier for the paying fans to swallow the enormous prices they were going to have to pay in order to watch him ply his trade.

"Being a Canadian kid," Joseph said, "it's exciting for me to play in Canada."

His former team, the Edmonton Oilers, new owners and all, were never in the bidding.

Exactly one week later, Peter Pocklington announced that he was leaving Edmonton permanently for California.

"I'd rather go where entrepreneurs are respected," he said. "I just feel that it's time to move on. Life is too short to stay where you're not appreciated. . . . Most people in Edmonton would be very happy if I left."

· THE GRIND ·

THERE ARE MANY WORSE ways to make a living than playing a kids' game and being paid loads of money, but yes, it is a grind. It is a grind for coaches, for players, for everyone involved. The National Hockey League season begins in early autumn with training camp, ends in April for the worst teams, late in June for the best. The travel alone can be debilitating. Unlike baseball teams, which spend three or four days in each city on the road, unlike football teams, which pack their bags once every couple of weeks for a day or two, hockey is a long series of one-night stands, stitched together by airplanes and airports and buses and hotels and dressing rooms. Travelling is not quite so tough for the New York Rangers, who are within a short hop of many of their Eastern Conference rivals, but it's extremely tough for the Edmonton Oilers, who aren't close to anywhere but Calgary and who, by virtue of their undercapitalized ownership, hardly travel in style. Get up, get on a plane, get to the rink, get on the ice, get off the ice to have something to eat, get back on the ice for a game, then back on a plane again. That's the players' life, the coaches' life, the life of trainers, of equipment handlers, of PR men.

Referees make the trips on their own, get booed in every arena, are screamed at by coaches and players, are noticed most when they make a mistake. General managers sweat it out behind closed doors, making endless phone calls, trying to satisfy the contract demands of star players enjoying the new freedom they've won through collective bargaining, trying to make the right deals at the March deadline that will set their team up for playoff success, trying to keep the owners at bay – even if that means sacrificing a coach they've hired. Agents struggle to keep their clients happy, to explain why an offer fell short of expectations, or why not playing hockey for a month or two or an entire season is the right strategy to secure riches down the road.

For all of them, there are days and nights when it's worth every aggravation. And then there are other days and nights, often late in the season, when the die is already cast, when playoff positions have already been established, when the life isn't quite so glamorous.

＊

ON A GOOD NIGHT in the National Hockey League, when the home team is winning, there is no shortage of heroes. The goal-scorers are naturally given credit, along with those who created the chances. A stalwart defenceman might not be as flashy, but if the opposition is stymied time and time again, the fans in the stands will certainly notice. Goaltenders are always in the spotlight, because in the end they stand alone against the shooters. A crucial save can win a hockey game, and when the three stars are acknowledged at the end, a goalie is very often among them.

On a bad night, the fans blame the coach.

Perhaps it's not quite that simple. Those who watch the game tend to understand the breakdowns, the missed checks or saves not made or shots missed, that can make the difference between winning and losing. But on those nights when nothing seems quite right, when the other guys are just, in some larger, all-encompassing sense, better, when the local heroes play like they'd rather be anywhere else but on the ice, the man behind the bench naturally is the focus of attention. Then, the coach is the window to the team's soul. He might be offering his players encouragement, if he still believes they have what it takes to win. He might be screaming at the officials, hoping to gain some kind of advantage, or just to vent his frustration. He might have turned on his charges, understanding that they've quit on him, that they know changing a coach is always easier for an owner than changing all of the players. He might be strangely serene, nearly comatose, understanding that his fate is a *fait accompli*.

Genius today, incompetent tomorrow. That's the way it goes for all of them, eventually. Pat Burns, hired and fired in Montreal, hired and fired in Toronto, was named coach of the year in both places before he outlived his usefulness. Ted Nolan, given the thankless task of taking over a Buffalo Sabres team that seemed desperately short of talent, won raves for leading his club to the playoffs. His reward – at the end of a feud that also cost general manager John Muckler his job – was to be fired soon after winning his coach of the year award. To his shock, he found that no one else required his services either, perhaps because other GMs were showing solidarity with their fallen brother. Blackballed wasn't too strong a word for it. Marc Crawford, hailed as one of the brightest young coaches in the game and given the honour of leading Team Canada at the Nagano Olympics, spent the final weeks of the 1997–98 season knowing that he'd be fired unless he won the Stanley Cup – and perhaps even then. Mike Murphy was merely the latest in a long line of coaches whose job it was to revive the Maple Leafs. At season's end, he'd have to wait weeks, in limbo, before finding out whether team president Ken Dryden planned to keep him around. Alain Vigneault was dropped into the most pressure-packed job in all of professional sports – coach of the Montreal Canadiens – knowing that Habs fans are satisfied only with

On the road to nowhere: Philadelphia Flyers general manager Bob Clarke (left)
and coach Wayne Cashman (right) made for uneasy seat-mates on a team bus,
shortly before Clarke fired Cashman in the middle of the 1997–98 season.

championships. Wayne Cashman's challenge in Philadelphia
was nearly as daunting. The Flyers had fired Terry Murray after
he'd taken the team all the way to the Stanley Cup Finals,
losing to Detroit. That made Cashman's mandate rather clear:
win a championship or else.

All of that on the line, and then try to get your team to the
finish, try to keep them motivated during the dog days of March
and April. It's a grind, because of the length of the season,
because of the pressure, because of having to explain yourself to
reporters every night, because if your players aren't good enough,
or they don't play hard enough, or your general manager isn't
patient enough, or your owner isn't committed enough, or it's
simply time for a change, you get fired.

"Coaches get fired because the teams don't win enough," says
Mike Milbury, who knows the territory well. He had his shot at
coaching with the Boston Bruins and now is employed on Long
Island as general manager of a struggling franchise. "This is a
very visible and erratic profession based on one thing – winning

and entertainment value. Part of the entertainment value is winning. And if you're not doing that, management and the ownership can't afford to keep going that way, because you'll lose people. And it's expensive to lose people's interest."

During the 1996–97 season, more than half of the head coaches in the NHL – 14 in all – lost their jobs, the highest rate of turnover in the history of the league. Coming down to the wire in 1998, in the weeks between the end of the Nagano Olympics and the beginning of the playoffs, several coaches knew their continued employment might well be on the line, while others, out of a job, waited in the wings for an opening to suddenly appear.

That's why coaches occasionally appear to lose their minds. That's why Crawford, soft-spoken, well-dressed, someone who likes to think of himself as a refined hockey man, could one night be seen jumping up and down behind the Colorado bench, his face beet red, looking to all the world like a three-year-old in the midst of a tantrum. He was screaming at the referee, "Too many. Too many. Too many. Goddammit, count the . . . guys!" because for a moment, the opposition had too many men on the ice, and nobody noticed.

Sometimes, there's nothing better to do than let it all hang out.

⤴

HOW DO YOU CONVINCE your players that a game they know isn't all that important is really a matter of life and death? How do you get them emotionally prepared to play when their thoughts might be elsewhere, when they're tired, when they're feeling the aches and pains brought on by all of those games, one after another, or are battling back from more serious injuries? What message do you offer when you know, in your

Stressing the point: Colorado coach Marc Crawford throws a tantrum, calling for a penalty for too many men on the ice.

heart, that no matter what you say, it isn't going to do a whole lot of good?

By the time the Washington Capitals played the Phoenix Coyotes in a late-season game in March, their fate had been pretty much decided. They would finish in the middle of the pack of Eastern Conference playoff teams. They would qualify for the post-season, their opening-round match-up decided as much by what others did as what they did. Brilliant play until season's end might move them up a couple of notches, and absolutely terrible play – combined with someone else's brilliant play – could conceivably cost them a playoff spot, but that wasn't going to happen. So in this game, they were just putting in time.

And they played like it. Through the first two periods, they went through the motions, leaving their coach, Ron Wilson, exasperated, but hardly at a loss for words. Some coaches say very little in the dressing room. Some coaches make very few words count. Some, like Scotty Bowman, the greatest coach of them all, prefer to play their head games in private, one-on-one, only occasionally putting on a public show when they think it might make an impact.

Wilson, though, thinks of himself as something of a motivational speaker. He likes to talk. He likes to stand in front of his team and make the 1990s' equivalent of the "win one for the Gipper" speech. Modern athletes are supposed to be immune to that kind of spiel, they're supposed to only be interested in where their next contract is coming from. But still, it's a game, a game they've been playing since childhood, a game they love, and so they aren't completely hardened. Who knows what these players will think this night, but Wilson is more than willing to take a shot. The button he pushes is a natural one. Jim Schoenfeld, the Coyotes' coach, used to be Washington's coach. Many of these same players played for him, and some of them didn't much like him – especially when he criticized their play on his way out the door. So even if this game lacks significance in the grand scheme of things, at least it might be a chance to settle old scores.

"If there's one or two games a year that I would expect a lot of guys in here to be motivated for, it would be the game that Jim Schoenfeld's involved in," Wilson begins. "I can't believe that you have the opportunity to show him that he was wrong if he did say anything and we don't take advantage of the opportunity. Actually, what we do is confirm what he was saying all along – that some guys don't want to play, that some guys don't want the puck, that some guys aren't physically involved. . . ."

His voice rises in anger.

"Jesus Christ, we lose tonight, Carolina wins, Carolina comes in here, they beat us, and then they're only six points back. We've just got to relax and play our game, and above all make a statement about what you are as a hockey player. This is what it's all about. This is what you want. Not easy games every night. You want tough hockey games. Isn't that right, Oatesie [Adam Oates]? You want every game to be the seventh game of the Stanley Cup Final. When you were little kids playing street hockey, isn't that what you pretended? I mean that's the way I look at it. I want every game, I want it all on the line every single night. I don't want an easy hockey game. Sure, for my heart and my stomach, it'd be nice to have easy hockey games. But you want games to count. And you want to show up when it counts. That's what I don't get. This isn't that big a game. What can I look for in the seventh game of the Stanley Cup Final if we ever get there? It's time for us to show up for 20 minutes and get the job done. Let's go!"

By the end, Wilson is nearly screaming. The players, having sat silently through the harangue, jump to their feet, perform a little ritual cheer of their own, and head to the ice for the third period, finally understanding their mission.

⁓

IT HAS BEEN A VERY good season for the St. Louis Blues, much better than many had expected, and naturally head coach Joel Quenneville is receiving much of the credit. His no-nonsense approach seems to have worked with a team that, so often in its history, has failed when expectations were at their height. But the Blues are certainly playing for him now. Superstar scorer Brett Hull has bought into the coach's system. Veterans and kids, stars and role players, have meshed together. St. Louis isn't the best team in the west during the regular season, but they're right up there, and a lot of observers see the makings of a great playoff team, what with Hull's scoring, and Grant Fuhr's goaltending, and a defence that features both the veteran Al MacInnis and rising young star Chris Pronger. Teams like this have a way of coming together during the spring tournament and winning at least a couple of rounds.

But this night, at venerable Maple Leaf Gardens in Toronto, the club's heart clearly isn't in it. And why would it be? The Leafs are a bad team, going nowhere. The Blues are better and know they're better and know this one game won't mean a whole lot in the grand scheme of things. Human nature suggests that a hockey team might just go through the motions in that situation every once in a while.

For a coach, though, that isn't an option. Even if his team rolls over in public, that's a reflection on his performance, a clear indication that he hasn't done his job, that he hasn't provided the necessary motivation. Behind the Blues bench, Quenneville is showing a heck of a lot more emotion than any of his players. He is apoplectic, and those sitting in the very expensive gold seats behind him are getting an earful through the Plexiglas.

"Would you guys . . . wake up, for Christ's sake here!" Quenneville bellows.

In the dressing room during the second intermission, with his team leading, he offers his own version of the pep talk. Though he and Ron Wilson have very different styles, the underlying message isn't all that different: please try a little harder, or at least look like you're trying a bit harder, because this is embarrassing me.

"That could have been our worst . . . hockey all year and we didn't lose the . . . period," Quenneville said, finding a ray of hope in the darkness. "So think of how . . . lucky we are and take advantage of it. But that was a horseshit . . . period of hockey. I don't know how many turnovers we had in our end and the neutral zone. I know the ice is horseshit. Let's do the simple things. Let's get . . . back in the game, boys. C'mon boys – it's right here if you want it."

And the Blues respond by . . . well, the truth is they don't respond much at all. They're still terrible. The Leafs dominate the period and tie the game. But as it turns out, the Blues are also terribly lucky. With the game tied and the final seconds ticking off at the end of the third period, MacInnis skates over the centre red line and sends a shot towards the Toronto net. MacInnis is known to have the hardest slapshot in hockey, perhaps the best since the glory days of Bobby Hull. But this isn't one of his best, more of a floater. Perhaps it dips, perhaps it's tipped. Somehow, it changes direction in a way that baffles Toronto netminder Felix Potvin. A goal scored from 60 feet away with 1.8 seconds to play, and the Blues escape with an undeserved win.

Quenneville knows they stole one as much as anyone. He's not about to pretend otherwise.

"Call the cops, boys," he yells after the puck goes in. "Oh my god. Call the cops. I've never seen it in my life. Holy . . ."

Afterward, meeting in private with his assistant, veteran coach Roger Neilson, Quenneville is considerably more subdued. The Blues got the victory, they got the two points in the standings, but there was nothing about their performance to suggest greater victories are in store down the road. Maybe it was a fluke, an off night, a natural letdown. Or maybe this St. Louis team really isn't that good. Quenneville can't answer that question right now, but he knows he'll have to very soon. If all doesn't go well during the playoffs, he'll have plenty of explaining to do – to the press, to the fans, to the general manager, to the owner.

"I can't . . . believe it," he says to Neilson. "What can they say after a game like that? They're going to have to shoot Felix. Jesus Christ, were we bad tonight." Quenneville starts rating his players' performance, on a scale of 1 to 10. "Duche [Steve Duchesne] was a one. [Chris] Pronger was one. He was awful. They can't play like that and accept it. Al MacInnis wasn't bad

St. Louis coach Joel Quenneville berates a video replay of his team's effort after an undeserved win: "Jesus Christ, were we bad tonight."

tonight. Pronger was so . . . bad tonight. Duchesne was awful. Jesus Christ. Al was not bad on defence. Bergie [Marc Bergevin] was brutal. [Darren] Turcotte was awful. I'm taking him out next game. He's done."

Neilson, who had stood silently, is moved to pipe up in Turcotte's defence.

"He didn't play that bad."

Quenneville will have none of it.

"He was awful. Throw that one in the garbage can for sure. That one was just awful. I never screamed so much on the bench. It was nuts."

˙ᴗ

QUENNEVILLE WAS AT least secure in the knowledge that this one terrible night hadn't put his job in jeopardy, that the Blues' season as a whole had made his continued employment in St. Louis relatively secure. (It is always relative, because there are always nasty surprises, and there are no sure things.)

Others in the same position wouldn't have that luxury. They were the ones standing behind the bench of teams that had performed below expectations – fans' expectations, owners' expectations, general managers' expectations – that may or may not have been based on the reality of the talent at hand. They had been unable to coax or encourage or prod or threaten their players into winning more often. They had been unable to devise strategies that might employ their personnel in a way that might give them a better chance of being competitive.

They were therefore on the firing line, because if coaches in hockey are anything, they are expendable. The quickest fix is a firing. The quickest way to deflect blame is a firing. The quickest way to make an old team look like a new team is a firing. The quickest way to convince players you mean business is a firing – though only rarely does a mid-season change make any appreciable difference.

Different people have different theories as to why NHL coaches are treated as disposable. One comes from Mike Keenan, whose act has played in Chicago, in New York (where he won the Stanley Cup), in St. Louis, and, by the middle of the 1997–98 season, was playing in Vancouver. He was speaking, however, during a brief period of unemployment, when, to kill the idle hours, he worked as a colour commentator for Toronto radio broadcasts of the St. Michael's major junior team.

"The reason why coaches are fired very readily in the NHL today is based on economic pressure and the fundamental lack of respect that the industry has for the coaches – more so, in my opinion, than any other major sport," Keenan said. "Basketball and some football coaches are paid very, very well, and for that reason they're a little bit more deliberate about dismissal."

Robin Burns agrees that money is part of the problem – but of course he would. He became the first coach's agent in hockey, negotiating his cousin Pat's deal with the Maple Leafs and subsequently being hired on by a host of other coaches eager to improve their bargaining power. "It's all about money," he says. "It's a big business. Sport is sport but professional sport is a business, so of course it's a bottom line [issue]."

Burns's goal has been to turn coaches into the same kind of commodity that players have become, to impress on owners their value, and to drive the salary market higher. If players can be measured by their goals and assists and penalty minutes, then surely hockey coaches' skills can be quantified and valued as well. "I guess you have to look at the guy's record, the longevity, what he has done percentage-wise," Burns says. "What he has done in the playoffs. The orchestration of the lines, was he able to match lines well, was he able to put a powerplay together that had a fairly decent percentage. His penalty killing strategies."

The average NHL player makes about a million dollars a year. The average coach makes about half of that, and only Scotty Bowman has so far has crossed the million-dollar barrier.

"Where should they be [on the salary scale]? I think they should be paid a minimum of halfway down your payroll," Burns says. "What's the average salary in the National Hockey League? Close to a million bucks now? And there's only maybe one coach that is touching that, and one or two that will be there in two or three years. They deserve a million dollars and some of the coaches deserve two million and three million – because I think that they are responsible in many cases for winning. And if the budget is not there because player X is taking it all, I think you're being penny wise and pound foolish."

And perhaps if they were paid that well, they wouldn't be

Unloved and underpaid? Scotty Bowman is still the only NHL coach to have broken the $1 million salary barrier.

quite so easy to fire. But as it stands, those in charge of a failing franchise will always look behind the bench for a scapegoat.

Rick Bowness understood early in the 1997–98 season that he might be the fall guy for what was happening with the New York Islanders. The once proud franchise had gone through tough times, had uncertain ownership, dwindling fan interest, and limited prospects. Even a series of high draft picks – the byproduct of a series of bad seasons – hadn't produced a winner, and the enforced retirement of Eric Lindros's brother Brett following a concussion hadn't helped matters at all.

Bowness had been fired before, in Boston, in Ottawa. At a post-game meeting with his boss, Mike Milbury, he could have been forgiven for feeling that the rug was being slipped gently from beneath his feet. The Islanders had lost again. They had not played well. And Milbury was offering his coach no protection.

"I didn't go to the game last night, but I've got to tell you I was a little perplexed. I had three different reports that were all off-the-wall different. . . . What the heck happened last night? I'm looking at you, you were there, you are the coach."

"I think it goes back to the expectations of the players . . ." Bowness began, but it was clear that Milbury wasn't really interested in his explanation.

"Players today are paid on market value," Bowness explained later. "They're not paid on their abilities any more. So if one general manager overpays somebody, everybody else benefits from it. Now you have players who don't deserve the amount of money they're getting, whether it's eight hundred thousand or two million. I'm happy that the players are making all this money, but now earn it. And don't make other people suffer because you're not making that commitment."

It is up to the coach to make those players play – though of course the team can spot a lame duck coach before anyone else can. So when Bowness pulled Jason Holland aside during practice to lecture him about his lack of effort, the words might not have had the desired effect.

"There's nothing assertive here, Jason. You're too good a player to be pushing yourself out of here. You should be challenging these . . . guys, and instead we're saying what the . . . are we seeing here. You piss some of these guys off, who gives a . . . You're fighting for a job here and unless we see you be more assertive, you're going to . . . Kentucky Friday morning. And I don't want to see that. I want to see you pushing through these . . . guys. . . ."

Fine, say what you want, coach, but it could be that you won't be here tomorrow. I'll take my chances with the new guy.

Early in March, Bowness was fired. Milbury stepped behind the bench to take his place for the remainder of the season.

AS STRANGE AS it might seem, success, even enormous, unexpected success, is not necessarily enough to protect a coach's job. At the beginning of the 1996–97 season, Ted Nolan was widely regarded as a sacrificial lamb. After all, who could succeed with the Buffalo Sabres? Their overall talent was perilously thin; their best player, Pat Lafontaine, was trying to come back from a concussion, against the odds. Their fans were unhappy; their ownership – burdened with the construction of a new arena – was cash poor. Any coach who took the job was a firing waiting to happen, a bit of insulation that general manager John Muckler could use to protect himself. Many preseason prognosticators had the Sabres pegged to finish at the very bottom of the league, and many thought Nolan wouldn't last much past Christmas.

What he did, instead, was write one of the better Cinderella stories of recent times. With Dominik Hasek coming into his own as the best goaltender in the league, and by convincing a group of grinders to play with grit and heart every night, Nolan's team finished atop the Northeast Division, with the third best record in the Eastern Conference. They beat Ottawa in the first round of the playoffs, before falling to the Philadelphia Flyers, who went on to the final.

But by the end of that remarkable run, the kudos for Nolan, including the coach of the year award, were already mixed with whispers that his job was in jeopardy. He and Muckler were barely speaking to each other. He and Hasek were on the outs, though it was never clear exactly what the problem was. The entire Sabres franchise was in flux, Nolan and Muckler appeared to be locked in a power struggle, and the betting was that only one would survive.

Neither survived. Muckler was fired. Nolan was fired. Eventually, the team's president was fired. All of this at the end of a season that had outstripped all expectations.

Immediately after his dismissal, Nolan's name began circulating in connection with vacancies here and there. After working wonders with the Sabres, surely he'd land a job. But the word was out. Any coach who appears to have turned on his GM risks the wrath of all the other GMs in the league. They rallied around Muckler, they froze Nolan out, and by the time the new season began, the previous season's coaching sensation remained unemployed. He spent his days with his family in Fort Erie, Ontario, waiting for a call. And he also took time to deliver a different kind of pep talk – like this one, in front of a group of native children in Northern Ontario.

"I lost my job last year," said Nolan, who is fiercely proud of his own native heritage. "I got the award as the best coach in the league – so they say. And all of a sudden next year you're not coaching. And that's really hard to understand. But you should never give up and never quit. And that's what I'm going to do now. I'm going to wait for another opportunity, another chance to coach again. And when I coach again, I'm going to be better. Just like when I was a little kid and I got cut from a team – I never quit then."

On October 26, the Tampa Bay Lightning fired their coach, Terry Crisp. The team's president, Phil Esposito, called Nolan and offered him the job. It would be a chance to try to turn around another sad-sack franchise with questionable ownership – a job tailor-made for Nolan, given the skills he'd demonstrated in Buffalo.

After some thought, Nolan said no. Jacques Demers took over the Lightning two weeks later.

"Financially, we were very close," says Nolan's agent, Robin Burns. "I said, Ted, are you sure? Are you really sure? And if you want my advice, I think you're really out of your mind not taking it."

"It's one of those situations where I'm a real big family-oriented guy, and I have to make sure the situation's right not for me alone," Nolan explains. "I said earlier I would coach anywhere, but now I'm taking my family into consideration, and with my two young boys, going down to Tampa Bay right now is not very good for them. They actually started crying on the couch. And a lot of people don't see that part of hockey – they just see job offers and opportunities. They don't see the human side of things. This was one of those situations where it just wasn't right now."

Entering the 1998–99 season, Nolan remained unemployed.

· ⌁

WHEN THE COACH has a bad day, the players feel his wrath, and when screaming at the players seems pointless, or when standing up for them seems the right thing to do, it's the officials who take their turn as targets. They are part of the travelling NHL road show as well, playing that same series of one-night stands. But for them, there's no glory, no celebration, no autographs. The men in the striped shirts must have days when they feel like no one's their friend.

Phoenix is playing Washington, Don Koharski is the referee, and Capitals coach Ron Wilson is all over him. Wilson has made a study of officials and their tendencies. He'll pull out a laptop computer to tell you who's tough and who's soft, who's tolerant and who's quick to boil. "I look at these things for misconduct penalties, for example," Wilson says. "Some referees are more prone to call ten-minute misconducts. You can talk to some guys and you can't talk to others. I think it's important for your players to know."

Koharski, obviously, is someone you can talk to, someone you can scream your lungs out at if necessary. "Take charge, Donnie! Why do you let it get to that? Why would you want to make a

Washington coach Ron Wilson tracks the penalty calls of individual referees with a laptop spreadsheet program, looking for their tendencies to favour particular calls.

decision? You'd have trouble in bingo." Koharski looks at the Washington bench and shrugs.

Then the Coyotes' Jeremy Roenick – JR by nickname – takes a run at Washington's Sergei Gonchar, flattening him into the boards. There is no penalty called, and Wilson is beside himself.

"What the . . . is that! Yeah, that's JR hockey. Donnie, wake the . . . up. How can he miss that? How can he miss that? Donnie, do you have a refereeing school? Do you have one? I'd come."

What kind of person would want to listen to that night after night, year after year? Who would want to be one of the 27 referees and 31 linesmen who make up the elite corps in the National Hockey League? The pay is decent, but who needs the abuse?

Bill McCreary has been taking it for 16 years. At age 43, he is the senior referee in the NHL, as widely respected as any current official. For him, refereeing was a way to remain close to the game he loves. "I played junior hockey in the seventies. I played major junior in Ontario as a 17-year-old and I didn't have the ability to continue on at a professional level. I got involved with minor hockey and officiating the younger children. The opportunity arose for me to continue on into the junior ranks. It's no different from being a coach or a player; you start at the minor levels and work your way through the American League and into the National Hockey League."

Each year, the officials go though their own pre-season training regimen, to prepare for the nights when they'll have to skate 15 kilometres during the course of a game. (The players play in shifts. The zebras never leave the ice.) "We used to come to training camp and get in shape at training camp, and work ourselves to a level of fitness that was acceptable. Now we're tested prior to training camp – we have to pass tests on and off the ice, and I think it's made a lot of our officials extend their careers. We have some officials now working into their fifties, which is a tremendous tribute to those people, and it's something the rest of us can strive for, to reach those goals."

Once the season begins, it can be a lonely life. Officials travel by themselves. They stay at hotels separate from the players and coaches, for obvious reasons. They socialize among themselves, or not at all. And their schedule is as daunting as anyone's, without the camaraderie of teammates to make it a little more tolerable. "There's lots of days you wake up when you're travelling and wonder where you are," McCreary says. "Last week I did Boston Monday, Pittsburgh Tuesday, St. Louis Thursday, Detroit Saturday. I was home Sunday and left for Tampa Sunday night. Worked Tampa Monday night, Miami Tuesday, was home yesterday and here I am in Chicago today."

All of that to have coaches, players, and fans constantly criticize your decisions, question your abilities, make you the focus

NHL referees have the loneliest grind in the game. Bill McCreary has been plugging away for 16 years.

when things go wrong. Since there's an aggrieved party most every night, the barrage is all but constant. Patience and tolerance, along with sure judgement, are obviously the referee's most important character traits. "We're humans, we make mistakes, and we don't win or lose," McCreary says. "Our job is to make sure the game is played safe and fair, whereas they have to win. If they don't win, it costs owners money and inevitably it costs coaches jobs and causes players to be traded. In the heat of the battle sometimes there are things said that I know they don't mean. But that's part of the game, too, and I think you've got to have some thick skin to accept that."

He takes it because, in the end, he loves it, he loves the game, he loves being part of it, he loves the flow, the speed, the excitement, he loves playing a role, even if it is often the villain's role.

"I think the greatest part is to be able to go on the ice and officiate professional athletes – the superstars, the great goaltenders, the great defencemen – and just the whole game of hockey," McCreary says. "I'm a big fan of hockey and I love being on the ice from the drop of the puck until it's over."

⁓

LARRY PLEAU IS ON the telephone. During much of the month of March 1998, Alexander Graham Bell's greatest invention has been Pleau's constant companion, all but permanently affixed to his ear. The latest call placed by the general manager of the St. Louis Blues is to his Vancouver counterpart, Mike Keenan, wondering if they might do a little business. Nothing serious, nothing hard and fast, just a little exploratory conversation. The NHL's trading deadline, the last time players can change teams before season's end, is five days away.

PLEAU: "Mike?"
KEENAN: "Yeah?"
PLEAU: "It's Larry Pleau."
KEENAN: "Hi, Larry. What did you sign Grant for?"
(The Blues have just signed their number one goaltender, Grant Fuhr, to a new two-year contract. Fuhr would have been eligible for unrestricted free agency at the end of the season, one of seven Blues in that situation.)
PLEAU: "Three one next year and then three the next year."
(That's three, as in three million dollars, U.S.)
KEENAN: "That's pretty good."
PLEAU: "Did you have any interest in him?"
KEENAN: "Yeah, I did."

The subject turns to Brett Hull, another of the St. Louis free agents. Hull wants six million a year over two years. The Blues have offered him five.

KEENAN: "Twelve million dollars? Where's he going to get twelve million dollars?"

PLEAU: "I don't think it's anything to do with them not wanting to say, Here. I think they just want to see what's out there. I offered him five [a year], so I'm . . . stupid, so maybe there's somebody that's worse than me."

KEENAN: "Boy oh boy, that's a lot of money."

That is indeed a lot of money. For players who become eligible to sell their services to the highest bidder without compensation, without restrictions, free agency represents a once-in-a-career bonanza, a chance to test the booming market for hockey talent. Deep-pocketed corporate owners in the United States have pushed the envelope. Expansion has increased the size of the marketplace. Star power sells tickets, big signings are news, and teams with small payrolls have a tough time winning Stanley Cups.

But if Larry Pleau gave all of his seven free agents what they wanted, his payroll would go through the roof, and his bosses, the team's owners, would fire him. It is a delicate, difficult business, part hard-headed, bottom-line decisions, part public relations exercise, in which hurt feelings can sometimes be as important as the sum total compensation in a contract. In addition, the ground is constantly shifting, the economics of the league are constantly changing.

For Pleau and his brother general managers, these last days before the deadline are the biggest test of the season. Deals can be swung that might win a championship. But on the other side, for teams that aren't going to win anything, salaries dumped now represent dollars that might be spent constructively in the future. And if veterans are bound and determined to test the free agent market, if they're going to leave town in any case, better to trade them away now and get something back, rather than lose them for nothing over the summer.

Pleau has signed Fuhr. His best offer has been rejected by Hull and MacInnis. The press and the fans are sensitive to any suggestions that the Blues might be losing their stars. And at the same time, the team has been playing well enough – because, it's been suggested, the potential free agents are putting out a little bit extra in anticipation of big contracts – that there seems a real possibility it could make some noise in the playoffs. There are two questions Pleau must answer: to deal or not to deal; to sign or not to sign. The clock is ticking, and no one is calling.

"I haven't had one phone call," Pleau says. "I've made phone calls but nobody's called me on it. I don't think it's there. They've seen what's happened in the past with Gretzky and [Ed] Belfour [late-season acquisitions who couldn't carry their new teams to a championship]. Teams are a little bit hesitant to pay a high price and say now we're going to win the Cup. Our team has played really well, and we feel we're competitive with any team in the league in a short series. And we still feel the same way. If we can get a player who can help us now and in the future, we'll look at it. But I don't see that happening."

Now, there are further complications. Hull has demanded a no-trade clause if he is to sign a new deal with St. Louis. Pleau has told him the team doesn't grant no-trade clauses, as a matter of policy. But then word leaks out that Fuhr, in his new deal, has been given the written assurance that he won't be dealt without his permission. The recriminations are flying.

The first to call is one of the Blues' broadcasters, who has gone on the air talking about how there are no no-trade deals in St. Louis, only to learn that he had been misled.

"I felt when we were on last night, there was nobody that had a no-trade clause, and I kind of felt stupid that Grant Fuhr had one apparently. . . ."

Let's make a deal: St. Louis general manager Larry Pleau speed-dialed his way through league front-offices in March 1998, looking for trades that might help reduce a payroll bloated by superstar contracts.

Pleau tries to mend fences.

"This was inherited when I got here. And I told his agent at the time when we started negotiating, we live up to whatever is in this contract because it was negotiated by the parties before I got here. . . ."

The reporter is miffed. Hull is furious. But that's not Pleau's only problem.

At a press conference, updating reporters on the negotiations, Pleau has inadvertently revealed MacInnis's contract demands. Players never like that kind of information discussed in public. It makes them look greedy. Even though Pleau only indirectly provided the numbers, MacInnis is seething. Over the phone, Pleau tries make amends.

"Al, how are you doing? What I said to the press – I did not detail your contract at all. I gave them figures that totalled different contracts, between Brett's and yours, and I told them that I compared yours as a comparable to Scott Stevens. And they figured out exactly what it was. There were no negotiations going on and I had to say something – and I apologize to you if you feel that it was too detailed. I said it right there in the press conference – these are two players that have earned the right to be a free agent. This is a once-in-a-lifetime situation. This is their chance to go into the free agent market. I respect that very much. I'm disappointed because we couldn't sign them because I felt that we offered dollars that would get them to the stage where they would be comfortable here. But I understand totally. I was a player at one time and I've got no problem with their decision. . . .

"You look at the hockey side and you look at the PR side," Pleau says after hanging up, hoping that MacInnis has been placated. "We screwed up on the PR side. One . . . little thing. I should have stood up in the press conference – and part of the whole thing should have been that if we ever inherited a no-trade contract, we'd have to live by it. It would have been simple. There would have been none of this today. Fifteen years ago in this business, nobody cared about PR and marketing. Oh shit . . ."

The press are starting to talk about turmoil in the locker room, about the distraction of the contract negotiations, about how the Blues management ought to be concentrating on keeping the players happy for the playoffs. Pleau, not surprisingly, doesn't buy that. "All year long all I heard was the reason our team was doing so well was simple – none of them have contracts. Now they're not going to do well any more because we've made such a distraction. We offered two guys 27 million and they refused it. That's a distraction. Why is that a disruption of the team?"

One more call, to the office of the Dallas Stars and their general manager, Bob Gainey.

PLEAU: "We haven't been able to sign Al MacInnis and Brett Hull."

GAINEY: "Uh-huh."

PLEAU: "And we've pulled the contracts off [the table]."

GAINEY: "Uh-huh."

PLEAU: "And we're not going to talk again until July. And I was just wondering if you had any interest in . . ."

GAINEY: "Where was MacInnis on his dollars?"

PLEAU: "We had offered four, four and four."

GAINEY: "Mm-hm."

PLEAU: "I thought that would be okay, too. I couldn't do all seven at one time. We did get Grant and we did get Jamie McLennan and Kelly Chase. But I was hoping to get one of them anyway."

GAINEY: "We wouldn't even be able to absorb part of that money so I think we would not be a serious player in that game."

PLEAU: "No?"

GAINEY: "No."

At the deadline, Pleau has received not a single offer for either Hull or MacInnis. He manages just one minor deal, unloading Harry York to the New York Rangers.

A few months later, cash-poor Bob Gainey will be singing a very different song.

·ᴗ

ALL OF WHICH PROVES that there has never been a better time to be a professional hockey player. Never before have the players been paid so well, never before have they enjoyed such leverage, never before have they been represented by so powerful a union. Where's the grind when you're making a million dollars a year to play a game?

From his office in Saskatoon, player agent Herb Pinder phones the New York offices of Neil Smith, the Rangers' general manager, telling him how much it's going to cost to retain the services of his client, goaltender Mike Richter.

"Neil? Hi. Finally. I think Mike was under the expectation that you were going to make your best offer. . . . This just comes directly from Mike. In the seven to seven five area [seven to seven and a half million dollars a year], I think there's a pretty good chance. It would be an easy decision."

A few minutes later, Pinder phones Richter with the good news.

"Guess who? I said it would be seven to seven five a year that was the range we'd probably be talking about. He didn't hang up, he didn't say one two, . . . you. He just said at least we know the playground. So my interpretation is that we didn't scare him off."

From the offices of the National Hockey League Players Association, lawyers gather round a speaker phone, the means by which Sergei Fedorov's arbitration case is being heard. Fedorov, a restricted free agent, sat out the first half of the season waiting for his previous employers, the Detroit Red Wings, or another team to make him an offer. Finally, the Carolina Hurricanes put something remarkable on the table, a deal structured to make the Wings – who retained the right to match any offer – balk.

The offer totalled $38 million over six years. Of that, $14 million would be paid immediately as a signing bonus. Should the Hurricanes make it as far as the conference final in 1998, a significant long shot in their case, Fedorov would be paid another $12 million. (If they didn't make the final, that money would be paid out over four years.) In other words, if the Wings matched the offer and played as they expected to play during the playoffs, they would owe Fedorov $26 million for one season of work.

The NHL challenged the validity of the Carolina offer. The Players Association, naturally, defended it. The matter went to arbitration. The Hurricanes and the NHLPA (not to mention Fedorov) won.

"Teams compete with each other," NHLPA president Bob Goodenow explains. "What Carolina did was put together an offer sheet that they thought would best allow them to have the opportunity to sign Sergei and have him play for them. That had these provisions for payment at certain times based on team accomplishments. And the league kicked it back because they wanted to protect their interests. Their interest is to keep player salaries down. The arbitrator looked at the case and said, in the context of the collective agreement, is this in violation of any of the provisions – and it wasn't. . . .

"For the Detroit people, it was an easy decision. They matched within a couple of hours. They had a player who they couldn't come to an agreement with in six or seven months, that they came to an agreement with in two hours once the offer sheet was there."

Fedorov returned to the Red Wings after missing the first 59 games of the regular season. He would be there when it mattered, and he would become a very rich young man.

How can it be a grind if you're being paid like that?

Perhaps, at $26 million, it can't be. But it can for others, for the Edmonton Oilers, playing out the final three-game road trip of a long regular season, every flight a long flight, nothing fancy, no frills.

"In the eighties, when the hockey club was as good as it was, I would have loved to see that club play in New York, or say, New Jersey or Philly," their coach, Ron Low, says. "Because I don't think that hockey club had any idea how many goals it could have scored if it wasn't tired some nights. We've kept our teams young for that exact reason. I don't think you can travel out here and be 35 or 34. It just doesn't work. It adds a big toll. You can kid yourself and they can kid themselves. . . . But definitely it does take a toll on players."

They blow a game in Anaheim. They fight back in Los Angeles. They end the season with a win against the Flames in Calgary and it's on to the playoffs. For Kevin Lowe, this is the last time he'll experience the end of the regular-season marathon. This is his 19th season in the NHL, his 15th with the Oilers. He has six Stanley Cup rings (five with Edmonton, one with the New York Rangers) to show for his efforts. He is 39 years old, and he has been hurt or sick for most of the season. Even now, he can't play two games in a row and finds himself trying to rest whenever he can.

"On the road, you really have one responsibility and one responsibility only," he says. "That's get to the rink and practise and play. Other than that it's downtime and you should take advantage of your downtime to rest up. Five games in seven nights or six games in nine nights – just because there are three days when you aren't playing doesn't mean that it's an absolute holiday. . . .

"I think it's supposed to be my last year. I want to give it a full shot at playing some games. But it's so hard to say. The best thing I've done over the last six or eight years was not think too much about the future and just think about the present."

And then there are those who would trade it all for a few meaningless games, another lousy road trip, a night in an anonymous hotel and a bad pre-game meal, for the grind. During the 1997–98 season, 82 NHL players were felled by concussions. Some weren't particularly serious, and the player was back for the next game (in the old days, when "getting your bell rung" wasn't considered serious, they would have been back for the next shift). Others missed weeks. A few missed months. Paul Kariya missed the Olympics, and the whole last half of the season after Gary Suter's crosscheck knocked him out. He didn't return until training camp the following autumn. Pat Lafontaine tried to come back with the New York Rangers, until one more blow to the head sent him to the bench, and eventually into retirement. Brett Lindros's professional career had barely begun when he had to call it quits. His brother Eric – who cried at the press conference announcing Brett's retirement – had his own scare late in the season.

Nick Kypreos, a tough guy employed by the Toronto Maple Leafs, got into a fight during a pre-season game against the New York Rangers on September 15. Ryan VandenBussche punched him in the head. He fell hard to the ice, lying in a pool of his own blood. For the longest time he didn't get up. It was a concussion, the Leafs announced the next day. Kypreos would be out for a week, ten days at the most.

"It was like I was constantly hung over, and you can't just shake it off," he says. "It's not like you sleep it off, or you wake up the next morning and just go about your business. It's kind of like an ongoing battle. You start off thinking it's a day-to-day thing, then all of a sudden your day-to-day becomes week-to-week and the next thing you know you're three or four months into it, and when is this going to end?"

While his teammates played out their season, Kypreos worked on his own, skating when he felt up to it on the empty ice at Maple Leaf Gardens. Game after game, he was listed as a scratch on the Toronto roster: post-concussion syndrome. The symptoms didn't go away. The hangover didn't lift.

"You always wonder if you'll be the same player you were before," Kypreos says. "I battled major knee surgery and shoulder surgery and I broke my leg last year. You always knew those things would heal, but when you're dealing with your head, you tend to think of the long-term picture. For me, the thought of a career ending at 32, it's a little more comforting to say than if

Down for the count: Despite making every effort to recover by working out, a concussion in a pre-season game derailed Leaf tough-guy Nick Kypreos's 1997–98 season, and ultimately ended his career.

I was 21 or 22 and just starting out and having to deal with this. I think of Brett Lindros and what he's going through. To have a head injury is just really tough."

At the end of the 1997–98 season, Nick Kypreos announced his retirement from hockey.

· THE FINALS ·

THE MOST STORIED TROPHY in professional sports comes with a price. The National Hockey League's regular season is an endurance test, a long string of one-night stands, of debilitating travel, of trying to put on a show for the fans and win the games and preserve enough energy to get to the end. It starts in October, ends in April, and puts players, coaches and everyone else involved through a physical and emotional pounding. That's what they get paid for – literally, in the case of the players, who receive all of their salary during the course of the regular season.

And then in the end, it turns out that none of that really matters. Only a handful of teams, the very bottom of the barrel, fail to qualify for the playoffs; it's a system that gives more players a chance at a championship, more fans a reason to care, and – just as important – gives more owners a chance to cash in on post-season gates. Everyone else prepares for what amounts to a separate, second season, one that can stretch another three months and, potentially, another 28 games. None of these will be walkovers, none of them will provide opportunities to take a breather, to coast through a shift or two. Playoff hockey is the best entertainment the sport has to offer, played with intensity, played with passion, and by-and-large played without fighting. To win the Stanley Cup, a team has to win four best-of-seven series, 16 victories to a championship. No other sport puts its clubs to such a test.

In 1998, the end of a historically long regular season (because of the hiatus for the Nagano Olympics) had produced no clear favourite to claim the prize. The defending champion Detroit Red Wings, though they finished the regular season with more points than they had the year before, seemed to lack the desperate will to win that had characterized their first Cup-winning campaign since 1955. The loss of defenceman Vladimir Konstantinov, brain-injured in a tragic off-season automobile accident, the aging of some of their stars, and Sergei Fedorov's long absence as he awaited a new contract made them seem vulnerable, or at least less of a team of destiny. And if they were to win the Cup again, they'd have to do it with Chris Osgood in goal. Veteran Mike Vernon had stepped in during the 1997 playoffs to carry the load and won the Conn Smythe trophy as the most valuable player of the post-season. Now he was gone to San Jose as a free agent, and though Osgood had played very well during the regular season, his propensity for occasionally losing concentration and letting in a soft goal made some wonder whether he could hold up under the pressure of the Stanley Cup tournament.

But if not the Red Wings, then who?

Perhaps the Colorado Avalanche, still stacked with the talent that had taken them to the Cup in 1996, still coached by Marc Crawford, still featuring Patrick Roy in goal, who had won championships all by himself. But the winds of discontent were already blowing around the franchise by the end of the regular season, including rumours that Crawford would be fired if the team didn't win a championship. Perhaps the New Jersey Devils, the 1995 champions. Playing Jacques Lemaire's defensively oriented system, they could shut more talented teams down at playoff time and sneak all the way to the finals. Perhaps Dallas, a team brilliantly built by Bob Gainey and well coached by Ken Hitchcock. Their regular-season success the past two seasons suggested they were on the verge of big things, and their playoff loss to the Edmonton Oilers in the first round the year before had no doubt been a growth experience. Perhaps even the Pittsburgh Penguins, who in their first season after Mario Lemieux's retirement surprised everyone by spending the regular season at or near the top of the conference standings. They, of course, had their own Czech Olympic hero in Jaromir Jagr, arguably the most talented player in the game.

The fans of all those teams thought they might win it, but the fans of only one team outside of Detroit felt that they should win it. In Philadelphia, Bob Clarke had built a roster that seemed destined to dominate the NHL in the last half of the 1990s. Eric Lindros was the linchpin, and around him there was plenty of talent – enough that the team had reached the finals the year before, only to be swept by Detroit. That experience could only make them better.

Still, two questions remained about the Flyers, one old, one new. The year before, the lack of a big-time playoff goaltender had helped cost the team a real shot at the Cup. Despite facing all kinds of pressure to make a deal, and despite the availability of some exceptional goaltenders (including Curtis Joseph), Clarke had chosen to stand pat in 1997, with Ron Hextall and Garth Snow. Late in the 1998 season he finally made a move, but not the one many would have expected, completing a deal with the Vancouver Canucks to acquire Sean Burke. Though once regarded as one of the best goaltenders in the game, Burke's reputation had plummeted in recent seasons, and his play in Vancouver had done nothing to suggest he was on the verge of a renaissance. Banking on him was a gamble – a curious gamble for a team that seemed so close to winning it all.

The other cause for concern in Philadelphia was Lindros's health. On March 7, not long after returning from the Olympics, Lindros suffered a concussion after taking a clean hit.

Eric Lindros was the linchpin of Philadelphia's 1997–98 Stanley Cup aspirations, but he would lead them only as far as an early playoff elimination by Buffalo.

The injury was a troubling echo of the concussion that had kept Paul Kariya out of the Olympics and ended his season, as well as the concussion that had ended the career of Lindros's younger brother, Brett. His injury would turn out to be not nearly so serious, but nevertheless he would miss 18 games, returning to action just four games before the playoffs began. Lindros said that he felt 100 per cent healthy, but doubts remained.

Everyone else in the post-season tournament could be considered an underdog, a long shot. Still, history had shown that, especially in the early rounds, upsets were a real possibility. A team riding a wave of emotion, or playing in front of a hot goaltender, could rise above its station and knock off a far more talented side. The playoffs were so long and so difficult that Cinderella teams didn't tend to last long enough to win the

Stanley Cup. But winning a series, or two, or even progressing right through to the finals was a real possibility if fortune smiled and the circumstances were right.

ᵕ

IN 1998, THE FIRST ROUND, as is so often the case, answered many of those outstanding questions about contenders and pretenders for the championship. One Cup favourite, the Red Wings, advanced past the Phoenix Coyotes, as expected. Another, the Dallas Stars, took care of the San Jose Sharks. No surprises there. Washington struggled, but still beat a Boston team that had to be happy just to advance to the post-season. The same applied to Larry Robinson's Los Angeles Kings, showing their first glimpses of hope in the post-Gretzky era but falling to the St. Louis Blues.

Beyond that, the 1998 Stanley Cup playoffs took a curious turn. For the second straight year, the Edmonton Oilers – at a time when the future of the franchise in Alberta was still on the line – orchestrated an enormous upset, knocking off the Avalanche in seven games after Colorado had taken a 3–1 series lead. The repercussions of that defeat in Denver would soon enough become apparent.

The Devils, who had seemed the perfect team to gain strength through the playoffs, looked old and slow against the Ottawa Senators, participants in the post-season for just the second time in their history. Down went another alleged Cup contender. In Montreal, the Canadiens partly redeemed themselves for a terrible playoff performance the year before by knocking off the Penguins – a triumph for their bright young coach, Alain Vigneault.

But the biggest story was written in Buffalo. Few franchises in any sport had survived the kind of turmoil the Sabres had

Former Oilers goaltender Ron Low orchestrated Edmonton's opening-round upset of Colorado in the 1997–98 playoffs.

gone through in the preceding 12 months. They had lost a general manager, lost a head coach, lost a team president, and seen the dressing room divided. But their new coach, Lindy Ruff, managed to heal those wounds over the course of the season, and by playoff time his team was playing well, was playing together, and most importantly was playing in front of the greatest goaltender in the world. Their victory over the Flyers was decisive, and no fluke – they had refused to be intimidated and beat Philly in every facet of the game.

At the end of the series, the sense of shock in the Philadelphia organization, from Clarke all the way down to Lindros, was clear for all to see. The club that was supposed to be The Next Great Team had taken a huge step back, leaving the clear impression that change had to come.

All of that added up to two very different scenarios in the NHL's two conferences. In the west, the Red Wings' path to the finals was a familiar one – first through St. Louis, and then through Dallas, where the Stars avenged their first-round loss to the Oilers the previous year by beating Edmonton to reach the conference final. The Wings would have to earn their chance to repeat as Cup winners.

In the East, the favourites had already fallen by the wayside. Whichever team emerged would head to the finals as an underdog against either Detroit or Dallas. The Sabres handled Montreal with relative ease, and Washington ended Ottawa's hopes, leaving two teams that had never won a Stanley Cup playing for the conference title, and that between them had made only one previous trip to the finals.

The two conference finals, the penultimate step to the Stanley Cup, couldn't have been more different. The Western powerhouses met head to head, Detroit versus Dallas, in the battle for supremacy that had been shaping up all year. In the end, the Wings' depth, their skills and the confidence built while winning the previous year made the difference in a tough, closely fought series.

On the other side, Buffalo had been that far only once, losing to Philadelphia in 1975. The Capitals, in their 25-year history, had never made it to the last round. Neither team was blessed with overwhelming offensive talent, though the Caps had to be granted a slight edge, because of Peter Bondra and Adam Oates. But the Sabres were used to facing teams with far more scoring power and beating them, thanks to Hasek. The series was framed as a battle of the goaltenders – Hasek versus Washington's Olaf Kolzig, who had played brilliantly during the playoffs – but in the end, the deciding factor seemed to be that Washington had a little bit more energy left, while the Sabres had spent themselves getting this far.

In the dressing room before the sixth and what turned out to be the final game against Buffalo, Washington coach Ron Wilson kept his message simple, while trying to impress upon his players the fact that they were on the verge of something special.

"What's wrong?" Wilson asked his players, in a light-hearted, mocking tone. "You're so . . . quiet. What's wrong? I don't have anything . . . funny to say. . . . Wake up."

Then, a final, four-word message.

"Skate. Fast. Hit. Win."

"C'mon boys," one player yelled. "Let's . . . end it tonight."

Off they went, and that they did. The Washington Capitals, underdogs, dark horses, the Cinderella team – all of the clichés applied – would play the defending champion Detroit Red Wings for the chance to hold high the Stanley Cup and temporarily call it their own.

⤳

WHILE THE ON-ICE DRAMA of the National Hockey League season played to its climax, the off-ice machinations continued. In the world of coaches, of general managers, of owners and scouts and players, those employed by everyone other than the two teams that would play for the Stanley Cup, preparations had already begun for the 1998–99 season and beyond. Most of the announcements wouldn't come until later, when there would be more opportunity to pique the hockey public's imagination during the quiet days of summer. But nonetheless, many of the significant decisions had already been made before the final game of the hockey year had been completed.

Later, much later, Brian Burke, the NHL's Director of Operations and the man so often in the spotlight when trouble arose, would explain that the Vancouver Canucks had called him after the last game of the finals to offer him the job of president and general manager. The opening had been created earlier in the year, with the surprise firing of Pat Quinn, and Burke had long been rumoured headed somewhere as a general

After leaving coach Mike Murphy dangling for weeks after the end of the 1997–98 season, Leafs president Ken Dryden (right) sacked Murphy and hired Pat Quinn (left), who had been dumped by Vancouver earlier that season.

manager. In Vancouver, his new task would be as daunting as his old job dealing with the league's evil-doers – work with control-freak coach Mike Keenan and turn a team of chronic under-achievers around.

After his firing, Quinn had picked himself up, dusted himself off, and signed on as coach of the Toronto Maple Leafs, replacing Mike Murphy, who had been left dangling for weeks after the regular season ended before he was finally fired by team president Ken Dryden. Quinn would be merely the latest to try to turn around that once proud franchise, a task made somewhat easier with the signing of free agent goaltender Curtis Joseph.

While there was discontent in Vancouver and Toronto, in Boston, the season could hardly have turned out better. The Bruins had gone from last overall the season before to a spot in the playoffs, better than anyone could have expected. In recognition of that accomplishment, Pat Burns was named the NHL's coach of the year, the first to manage that feat three times with three different teams.

For the Bruins' two prized first-round draft picks, the early reviews in training camp had proven prophetic. Joe Thornton, the number-one draft pick overall, stuck with the team for the entire NHL season, avoiding being returned to the juniors. But he struggled to look like he belonged, never played a regular shift, and finished the season with just three goals. Thornton was clearly a long-term project. That was especially obvious when he was compared with Sergei Samsonov, who proved that his strong early showing was anything but a fluke. He had been a major part of the Boston resurgence, finishing the season with 22 goals and 25 assists. On the same night Burns won his award, Samsonov won the Calder Memorial Trophy as the NHL's rookie of the year. In his speech, he dedicated the prize to his father, who had moved his family from Russia to North America so Samsonov could pursue his dream of a professional career.

During those same awards, Dominik Hasek, the Sabres goaltender and the Olympic hero, for the second straight year won both the Vezina Trophy as the league's best goalie and the Hart Trophy as its most valuable player.

Brett Hull, who had caused such a stir with his assertion that "the game sucks" and who was almost traded away by the St. Louis Blues during the season, took advantage of unrestricted free agency to sign a three-year, $17-million deal with the Dallas Stars, a move the Stars hoped would help them take the final step to a Stanley Cup.

The other major signing of the off-season would come only after persistent rumours that Eric Lindros was on the trading block, not to mention intentionally provocative on-the-record statements from Bob Clarke that if Lindros expected to be paid like the best player in the league, he'd better produce like the best player in the league. Finally, Clarke and Lindros's father and agent, Carl, came to an oral agreement on a one-year, $8.5-million deal that would keep Lindros with the Flyers for at least another season, setting up the same pressures and expectations of greatness that have followed him every step of his career.

"It has been amusing, frustrating, whatever adjective you choose," Milbury says. "That's the hockey world, that's the cycle of life in hockey. Entertaining, yes – not just on the ice, but off."

In June, out of the blue, Pierre Gauthier, the bright young general manager of the Ottawa Senators, the man who could claim much of the credit for leading that team to respectability, quit the post – because, he said, he wanted to spend more time with his family. There were rumours that what Gauthier really planned to do was move to Anaheim and take over the operation of the Mighty Ducks from Jack Ferreira. At his farewell press conference, Gauthier denied that was the case.

"I'm not going to Anaheim," he said. "Not to work for the Mighty Ducks. I do not have the right to steal anybody's job, and I wouldn't do that to anybody, and certainly not to Jack Ferreira."

Six weeks later, Gauthier, the new president of the Mighty Ducks, demoted Ferreira and named himself general manager.

The most significant executive decision in the NHL, though, was one that, in the end, didn't result in any change. After thinking about it long and hard, and meeting with the new owners of the team, Glen Sather decided to stay with the Edmonton Oilers. His continued presence suggested that, despite long odds, the team had a real chance of surviving in Alberta. "What I'm really worried about in the future is whether we can remain competitive, not on the ice but when we start to write cheques," Sather said. "I'm speaking from a Canadian point of view. We're all handicapped."

As for the game, rather than the business of the game, Sather felt the past year had been a success. "There's been a lot of change, but a lot of good change. If there are any prob-

In June 1998, Ottawa general manager Pierre Gauthier abruptly quit, denying rumours he was going to Anaheim to take Jack Ferreira's job. "I wouldn't do that to anybody," he vowed. Six weeks later, he went to Anaheim.

lems, we've seen what they are and we're going to rectify them. And if we do that, then maybe we can survive for another hundred years."

There was nothing really out of the ordinary in all of that, the usual off-season shuffle, the big money deals, the bold moves that signalled which teams were serious about trying to win a Stanley Cup in the near future and which were just treading water. Some of the specifics might have been a surprise, but the pattern of hirings and firings is the same every year.

What happened in August, though, nobody anticipated.

It had, all agreed, been an exceptionally difficult season for the National Hockey League. Television ratings were down across the board. Stars were complaining about the level of play. Marquee players were felled by concussions. Small-market teams in Canada were saying that they couldn't hold on much longer under the current system. The Olympic experiment, despite all its promise, hadn't worked out as the league had hoped it would. Though expansion was proceeding as planned,

*After the sale of the Edmonton Oilers to a community-based consortium, team
president and general manager Glen Sather surprised many by deciding to stay on.*

hockey seemed headed for some troubled times.

And then, in August, Gary Bettman made the most significant announcement of his tenure as commissioner and one of
the most significant in the history of the league. The Disney
Corporation, owners of the Mighty Ducks, would pay $600
million for the right to televise NHL games for the next five years
on ABC and ESPN. The deal represented an extra $4 million
(U.S.) a year for each team over and above what they'd been
receiving from the previous deal with Fox. "This, from our standpoint," the commissioner said while making the announcement, "is a marriage made in heaven."

It wasn't hard to read the sentiment behind Bettman's smile
that day: "Problems? What problems?"

·➴

THROUGHOUT MOST OF THEIR 25 seasons in the National
Hockey League, the Washington Capitals had seemed like a

team from nowhere, without a discernible personality, a club as bland as its uniforms, one that, year in and year out, seemed capable of making virtually no impact, on or off the ice. (That's saying something when you consider that even the long-dead California Golden Seals had their legacy, if only thanks to the eccentricities of owner Charlie O. Finley.)

The Caps had come into being as a result of the NHL's fourth expansion, following on the heels of the great leap forward with the addition of six teams in 1967, the birth of the Buffalo Sabres and Vancouver Canucks in 1970, and the addition of the New York Islanders and Atlanta Flames in 1972. The league added two teams in 1974 – the Kansas City Scouts (who moved first to Denver, and then to New Jersey, where as the Devils they won the Stanley Cup in 1995), and the Capitals, who played in a rink located in Landover, Maryland, outside the beltway that defined the real Washington, outside the city proper, at the geographical centre of nothing.

The capital of the United States has been a half-hearted sports town for most of its history. The Redskins of the National Football League are supported passionately, and tickets for their games are at such a premium that even the movers and shakers of the government needed further connections to gain entry to the stadium. But at the same time, Major League Baseball in the city had died not once, but twice, as two different generations of Senators had been forced to leave for lack of interest. The city's NBA franchise, the Wizards (formerly the Bullets), has sometimes been well supported. But hockey, as far as anyone could tell, had no place in the local public imagination.

It didn't help that the Capitals were dreadful from their inception, in their first season the worst team in the long history of the NHL, finishing with a record of 8–67–5. Even as the franchise eventually crawled out from under expansion awfulness, it seemed cursed, especially compared with the Islanders, who would win a string of Stanley Cups and long be held up as a model organization. When the Capitals appeared close to a breakthrough, when they put together a squad that seemed capable of winning, one terrible playoff letdown followed another.

That changed with a move to a new, downtown arena, the MCI Center, and especially with the arrival of Ron Wilson to coach the team in the 1997–98 season. Wilson is the son of Larry Wilson, a fringe NHL player and a minor league coach whose one shot at the big time came when he was given the job of coaching the Detroit Red Wings midway through the 1976–77 season. The Wings were terrible before and after Larry Wilson took over, compiling a record of 3–29–4. That was the sum total of his NHL coaching career: the next year, he was back in the minors to stay.

His son excelled as a university player, a defenceman with very good offensive skills. He was drafted and began his career with the Toronto Maple Leafs, finishing it with the Los Angeles Kings 177 games later.

Though he never really made an impression as an NHL player, as an NHL head coach Ron Wilson was an immediate success, taking the helm of the expansion Anaheim Mighty Ducks and leading them to the second round of the playoffs in just their four seasons of existence in 1996–97, when they took the Red Wings to overtime in three games before losing to the eventual Stanley Cup champions. Wilson took time out from his Anaheim duties to coach the United States to victory in the first World Cup of hockey and later was chosen to coach the ill-fated U.S. team at the Nagano Olympics. Any list of the best coaches in the National Hockey League would include his name – something even those put off by his sometimes aloof, cocky manner would be forced to admit.

That said, by the end of the 1996–97 season, the greatest year in the Ducks' short history, Wilson and the Mighty Ducks' owners, the Disney Corporation, weren't seeing eye-to-eye. He was too outspoken for them, a little too flamboyant, not enough of the kind of good company man the corporation so valued. To the surprise of many in hockey, the coach and team parted company, immediately making Wilson the leading candidate for every open job in the league.

The Capitals' new general manager, George McPhee, snapped him up, eager to finally find a way to advance in the playoffs and eager to put a new, positive face on the featureless team as it moved into its new arena. Wilson's club didn't blow anyone away during his first regular season in Washington and was generally regarded as one of the league's disappointments, given the decent level of talent on the roster. But they qualified comfortably for the post-season, and in the playoffs, perhaps thanks in part to the fact that the Eastern favourites had immediately fallen to the wayside, they got better with each series, riding the goaltending of Olaf Kolzig and a disciplined, team approach all the way to the finals.

Simply by getting there, they had accomplished something that no other Capitals team had done. "We were always fearful as a team of that so-called Washington curse," Wilson says. "It just seemed as we went along, every time we got to that position of being up three to one, we could hear this negative drum beat in the background. . . . You can't win the Stanley Cup unless you get to the finals. That's one of the things we found out along the way. It's just the greatest feeling in the world – I think – next to winning the Stanley Cup."

When it sunk in that they would actually be playing for the Stanley Cup, the veteran players, especially, were caught up in the moment. "It's an emotional time," Wilson says, looking back to those weeks. "You see [Dale Hunter], this real tough guy

The Washington Capitals celebrate Joey Juneau's overtime goal, which propelled them into the 1997–98 Stanley Cup finals. At last, the Washington curse of playoff collapses appeared to be over.

who doesn't say boo breaking down with tears coming down his cheeks. I thought to myself, boy, often you don't realize how much this means to other people. You're caught up in your own little world of how much it means to you getting to the finals."

On the wall of their dressing room, Wilson had pinned up a calendar that counted down from 16 to 0 – 16 being the number of playoff victories it takes to win the Stanley Cup. With the triumph over Buffalo, another page came down, and the number changed from five to four. "When we tore the number off, you say, boy we've really accomplished something," Wilson says. "We're one of only two teams left."

But however sweet, those same emotions, that sense of accomplishment was a problem that Wilson and his players had to overcome. It had been without question a tremendous achievement. They had finally beaten the Washington curse.

They were only four wins away from having their names engraved alongside all the others. The problem was that over in Detroit, the players weren't breathing big sighs of relief, they weren't wallowing in the accomplishment of just being there. The Red Wings didn't have the option of settling for moral victories. They wouldn't let down, not until the task was finished.

Tactically, Wilson was as solid as any coach in the NHL. But he considered the emotional part of the game his specialty and wasn't afraid to try something a little out of the ordinary. During the playoffs, he'd screened movies for his players that he thought might be inspirational, *The Wizard of Oz* during the Boston series, and *Apollo 13* before they played Ottawa. So often, in hockey as in all sports, in the end the Xs and Os didn't much matter. Things much harder to quantify than talent, things like desire and passion and effort, represented the difference between winners and losers. Heading into the Stanley Cup finals as prohibitive underdogs – so much so, that many hockey insiders were openly predicting a Detroit sweep – Wilson understood that he had his work cut out for him. If the Caps were to have any chance, they'd have to rise to a new level of intensity, they would have to play above themselves, they couldn't be intimidated by their adversaries, and most of all they had to forget the tremendous sense of relief that had come with beating the Sabres to get this far.

"The better coaches aren't afraid to be a little unconventional in terms of motivating people," Wilson says. "Being a parent I think I understand 18-, 19-, 20-, 21-year-old people as well as anybody. Some need pats on the back and some need kicks in the rear. You have to be able to motivate individuals and you also have to paint a big picture for the whole team. . . .

"If I could ever get close to being the kind of leader that George Patton was, getting the most out of his men, then that's the kind of a person I'd want to be. To be that strong in the face of adversity."

So what do you tell a collection of kids and veterans, impressionable teenagers and grown-ups, some of whom appreciate the moment, some of whom don't really get it? How do you preserve the confidence, the magic, that had built over the past three series?

At the beginning, Wilson decided, by helping them to relax, to enjoy themselves, by taking the pressure off. "Is this fun or what?" Wilson hollered during the last practice before the first game of the finals. "You always figured hockey in June, that's got to suck, but this is pretty good."

Wilson even invited his players to his house for a pre-finals pool party, along with their wives and children. "The best way for a coach to put perspective back into things is to stage an event where he sees a guy interacting with his teammates away from the arena, sees a guy interacting with his kids away from the arena. Then you remember that they're people and that you have to treat them like people."

Beyond that, there were quiet, private conversations with individual players, trying to strike the appropriate chord. "You'll be the first Slovak with your name on the Cup," Wilson said after pulling aside Peter Bondra, the most talented offensive player on his team. "You've got to do it, man. You never know. This could be your last chance. I hate to say it that way, but you have to assume this might be the only chance you get."

For Wilson, reaching the finals also represented a personal achievement, as it would for any coach. "I've never had a dream where I was coaching in the finals, but you always wonder what it must be like. I always thought that it must be one heck of a marathon and you'd be completely exhausted by the time you get to this position. But it hasn't felt like that at all. Winning is a great elixir. Actually, as you go through this, you feel younger."

Especially significant for Wilson was who was coaching the opposition. Before the series began, he said, "I've coached against Scotty Bowman before. He's the greatest coach of all time. That makes this even better. You want to be the best; as a team you want to play the best. As a coach you want to face the best coaches. I'm going to enjoy this, that's for sure. I'm not going to go into this and not enjoy it. This is a time of your life that you should enjoy."

Of course, Wilson and the Capitals weren't there just to enjoy themselves. They were there to win the Stanley Cup, a task that the coaching staff understood would be daunting. "The bottom line is that we understand we're playing the best team in the league, and it's going to be infinitely more difficult than the last three series were. And that's how we'll approach it," Wilson said. "I think in the first game we're just going to let the chips fall where they may and see what we need to do. We don't want to go into the first game and do something that's not going to work or that fails; we're second-guessing. We'll make adjustments as the series goes on."

That wasn't what he'd say to his players, though. That was the kind of thing coaches said to other coaches. In the dressing room before the game, he would try to convey a simple message that would send his team onto the ice confident, emotionally high, and ready to meet the challenge ahead.

"I think coaches are storytellers as well," Wilson says. "They need the ability to paint a picture for the players and simplify things and keep things somewhat light-hearted, especially when we're talking about serious matters."

For Game One of the Stanley Cup finals, the story he chose to tell was one of a team facing a difficult challenge, and of a team that perhaps didn't yet realize just how good it was. It would be an intimidating proposition beginning the series at Joe Louis Arena, the Red Wings' home. It would be an intimidat-

Washington coach Ron Wilson rallies the troops in a dressing room speech before Game One of the 1997–98 Stanley Cup finals.

ing proposition facing the defending champions, especially for a room full of players who had never been that far before. So Wilson tried to diminish the Detroit mystique, to level the playing field, to assure his players that they really belonged in the finals, even though many outside the team were openly doubting their credentials. *Those guys on the other bench – they're just like us.*

"We've lost five games in the playoffs so far, and won twelve," Wilson said in the dressing room a few minutes before the puck was dropped for the opening face-off. "They've lost six and won twelve, too. Phoenix and St. Louis, teams that aren't as good as us, came in here and beat them in Joe Louis Arena. And then they fell apart as the series went on under the pressure of the Red Wings. If we're going to lose this series, it's going to be in six or seven games. But I don't think that's going to happen at all. I think we're going to win the series. It's that simple. I think everybody in here believes that too. . . .

"I think in this room everybody knows how good we are, and that's all that really matters. It's not what anybody else thinks. They don't get it. A lot of people haven't got what we've been trying to do all year but we get it and that's all that really matters."

It was a very good speech. But then the team left the dressing room and skated onto the ice for the first game of the 1998 Stanley Cup finals, and Wilson's words evaporated in the intensity of the moment.

"I don't think our team felt it until we went out, with the introductions and the camera light literally right in your face," Wilson says. "The whole atmosphere. Looking across and knowing that you're playing for the Stanley Cup. I think that it hit us in the face like a cold facecloth. I think that our team went out there honestly really truly believing that we were a team of destiny, that we were going to win the Stanley Cup."

If their confidence was shaken by the scene inside the arena, it was shattered during a two-minute stretch late in the first period. Teams that score first in the NHL win about 70 per cent of the time. The team that scored first in this series would feel a huge surge of confidence – the Caps, because they might start to believe that they really had a chance to win, the Wings because it would be a sign that the history of a year before was about to repeat itself.

Fourteen minutes and four seconds into the opening period, Joey Kocur took a backhand pass from Doug Brown in the slot and tipped the puck past Olaf Kolzig. Joe Kocur, a fourth-line player, a year and a half earlier had been out of pro hockey all together, playing in a recreational beer league, and was added to the Detroit line-up only because Brent Gilchrist had been injured.

Behind the Washington bench, Wilson worked desperately to pump up his players' sagging confidence.

Washington coach Ron Wilson (left) strove to match lines and wits with Detroit's Scotty Bowman (right), a master manipulator, in the 1997–98 Stanley Cup finals. It was a time for hard thought.

"A little enthusiasm, gang! We're in the finals! We don't have enough guys here who look like they believe we've got this one!"

"If you're down 1–0, players start to feel a sort of antsiness," Wilson said. "We've got to score the next goal."

Then Nicklas Lidstrom beat Kolzig from the point, and Detroit was leading 2–0.

The Caps were shell-shocked, and even though they got a goal back in the second period from Richard Zednik, everything about the game suggested their destiny was sealed. It finished 2–1 Detroit, with the Red Wings outshooting the Capitals 31–17. In the end, Washington had played very well, they hadn't folded under pressure, and in their previous series, it probably would have been enough to win. But not against this level of opposition.

"We got it back to two to one, and we couldn't tie it up," Wilson said afterwards. "That's what scares me most. Because after that it was like this light went on – we're playing the Detroit Red Wings. They're much better than us. It's not Buffalo. It's not Ottawa. It's not Boston. We're not going to beat this team."

No one understood the situation better than Bowman, a master of the psychological side of the game himself, someone whose players tended to hate him but also tended to win for him, someone whose opponents invariably hated him, and then more often than not wound up on the losing end. Bowman had shown in the past that he would do whatever it took – baiting players, screaming at referees, confronting a team bus, or saying nothing at all – to get under the other guys' skin.

At the post-game press conference, Bowman picked his moment and then sent a message directed at the heart of the Washington Capitals.

"I think that Washington played a real good game for their first game in the finals," he said. "And we have got to do a lot better than that."

"I think our team was really discouraged and Scotty's remarks reinforced that," Wilson says. "He said, 'We didn't play very well.' That's what put the fear of God or the fear of Scotty into our players. They knew the Red Wings were going to play better, and we weren't sure that we could play much better than we had in the last two periods and we still couldn't beat them."

Wilson sent out his own message through the press, telling everyone that his Caps weren't conceding. "If we lose tomorrow, we're down two nothing in the series. Obviously, playing a team like Detroit, that's going to be difficult to come back from. But I don't believe in my heart that it's impossible."

Now he had to convince his players of that.

At Washington's skate on the morning of Game Two, Wilson returned to some of his earlier themes.

"We had too much respect for them the other night," he said. "We weren't yapping at them from the bench. By yapping at them we show that we don't respect them – we respect them, but we don't respect them. We think we can play with them. Let's just come relaxed, ready to play and have some fun. And realize, truly believe here, that we can beat this team. Screw me, we're in the finals here. And it's not by luck, like everybody wants to say. We beat some pretty good teams. Now obviously Detroit is the best team in the league. But come ready to play tonight, come believing that we're going home with a split, and then we take charge of this series."

That night in the dressing room, in the minutes immediately before the Capitals took the ice, he decided that something different, more elaborate, more complex was in order. Acknowledging their underdog status, acknowledging that no one in the hockey world thought that they were going to beat Detroit, Wilson tried to use the team's predicament to stir their emotions. "Us against the world" was the subject of his second sermon of the finals, but placed in an unusual, surprising context.

"Do you know what a *hambla chiapi* is?" Wilson began. "Si? [directed to Chris Simon] Chief? [and to Craig Berube – the two Capitals who are of Native American heritage] It's an Indian word. It's Lakota Sioux. A *hambla chiapi* is a vision, and an Indian, a warrior, a guy like Crazy Horse would dedicate himself to that vision and dream. We're obviously a group of warriors here and we're heading into battle. Crazy Horse had a saying that he picked up in this dream. His saying was *hanta yo*. And it meant 'It's a good day to die.' Ours will be 'It's a good day to lose.' We have to play today's game, we can't be afraid to lose. So we go out there and pound on the Detroit Red Wings tonight, we don't show them any respect. And if we're not afraid to lose the hockey game, we'll all come in here winners in the end. Courage and spirit in battle. We go out there, give it our all, we're not afraid to lose, we'll all be . . . better for it."

A stretch, perhaps, but judging by what happened next, there's every reason to believe that it worked, that taking the ice for Game Two, the Capitals had renewed faith in themselves; they had recaptured much of the confidence that had grown over the first three rounds of the playoffs. The Wings scored early to take the lead and dominated the first period, with no more scoring from either side. But this time Washington fought back, tying the game on Peter Bondra's goal, and then taking a 2–1 lead when Chris Simon scored, and then a 3–1 lead, when Adam Oates scored at 11:03 of the second. They carried that lead into the second intermission. Kolzig had been brilliant. The Red Wings seemed shaken. The possibility of the series returning to Washington tied 1–1 seemed very real.

"I thought for sure we were going to win the hockey game," Wilson says. "We played very well for two periods. Olie was very good again. We got some great goals. I remember Adam Oates's goal – he stole the puck and went in and put it in the top shelf. An incredible move and an incredible goal. And I thought, we're doing it. We're relaxed. We're not afraid of losing."

Then the third period began, and the Wings found another gear. "When Detroit came out in the first five minutes, we sort of weathered the storm, but they never stopped and we got intimidated," Wilson says. "They made it 3–2, we made it 4–2, then they made it 4–3."

The turning point of the game, and perhaps the turning point of the series – or at least the moment when Washington still might have had a chance to make it interesting – came in the middle of the third period.

"In the middle of a change, Esa Tikkanen steals the puck and he goes in alone," Wilson remembers. "He made a great move and he missed the net. And it was like we lost. I can't describe how our bench sunk, and yet we were up 4–3. It's one of those

*It's over: When Esa Tikkanen missed a wide-open net in Game Two of the
1997–98 finals, the Capitals caved in. "It was like we lost," Ron Wilson
recalled. "And yet we were up 4–3." They lost in overtime, 5–4, and never
seriously challenged Detroit again.*

things that anybody who coaches or anybody who's a parent
understands. Our team was defeated at that moment. It didn't
seem as if anything I said was going to matter. I came into the
room and I was looking into their eyes and trying to get a feel.
Without the look, we weren't going to win the hockey game."

And without this hockey game, they weren't going to win
the Stanley Cup.

Detroit's Doug Brown scored moments after Tikkanen's miss,
tying the game 4–4 with 4:14 to go in the third. "I tried to rally
the troops," Wilson says. "I told them, this had happened before,
this had happened in Game Two against Buffalo. But in this
overtime game we weren't even close. It just seemed inevitable
that the Red Wings were going to score, and they did."

After Kris Draper scored the game-winner for the Red Wings

15:24 into overtime, Bowman shook his fist in celebration behind the Red Wings bench. It was the gesture of someone who has won enough championships to know when another one is within his grasp.

Afterwards, the Caps said all the things that teams down 2–0 in a best-of-seven series always say. "We've just got to win at home," Kolzig told reporters. "It's the old saying. You can't take your foot off the snake's head. We had them down 4–2 and then had a chance to make it 5–3. Then we let the snake get up and bite us. Time and time and time again we've bounced back. So let's see how we do on Saturday."

"There's a lot of positive things we'll pull out of it and we'll bounce right back at home," Wilson said. "We have to win one game in Detroit. If it takes four tries to do it, so be it. We'll bounce back at home."

In his heart, and in his head, Wilson understood how unlikely that was.

·◡

DURING THE FINALS, the Stanley Cup itself goes on the road, to be put on display in the competing cities, where the fans can get close enough to read the engravings. Of course, it had never been to Washington before 1998, except when the victorious Red Wings brought it to the White House for their visit with President Bill Clinton the year before. And even if there weren't huge line-ups waiting long into the night for a glimpse, as there have been in other cities at other times, the Cup was certainly more than a mere curiosity. For the first time in its quarter-century hockey history, the city seemed fully turned on by the sport. A chance to win a championship will do that, even if by the time the Capitals and Wings took to the ice for Game Three, that chance had been reduced considerably.

For inspiration in the 1997–98 finals, the Red Wing players didn't have to look far. Vladimir Konstantinov, severely injured in a car accident, was watching from the stands.

If Detroit needed any added inspiration to augment their clear advantage in talent, they didn't have to look far. In the stands, watching the game at the MCI Center would be Vladimir Konstantinov. His injuries had largely confined him to a wheel-chair, had restricted his ability to speak, had left him a physical shell compared to the big, strong defenceman who had been a cornerstone of the 1997 championship team. Even being in the arena represented a triumph, and teammates, knowing that, knowing he was there, had another reason to win. Wilson, still desperately trying to find some kind of psychological advantage, knew that he was overmatched. "There is nothing in my bag of tricks I could use to go where the Red Wings could go in terms of emotions with Vladdy Konstantinov," he said.

Before Game Three, the Washington players heard a pep talk of a different sort. Abe Pollin, who had owned the franchise since its inception, made a rare appearance to offer his thanks. Soft-spoken and gentlemanly, he clearly spoke from the heart.

"Gentlemen, gentlemen, gentlemen. How are you all doing tonight?" he began. "I just want you to know how proud I am of what you've achieved. This is the first time that a Stanley Cup final is being played in the nation's capital, the most important city in the world. That's due to you. It's an absolutely unbelievable achievement to bring us to where we are and I know you're going to keep going and we're going to win the Stanley Cup. What I want to do is wish you well, and after the game tonight I'll be back here to congratulate all of you. Go get 'em. Go get 'em."

For his part, Wilson abandoned tales of mythic warriors during his third sermon in favour of down-to-earth hockey macho rhetoric.

"I was just watching TV," he said. "They call one of our lines the Capital Punishment line. What does capital punishment mean? What's capital punishment?"

After a short pause, one of the players piped up with an answer.

"Death," he said.

"Death," said Wilson, taking his cue. "The death penalty. So it's the death penalty on the Detroit Red Wings, in other words. Capital punishment. Is that what this is? Then let's start with capital punishment then. Hunts [Dale Hunter]. Chief [Craig Berube]. Si [Chris Simon]. Tinner [Mark Tinordi]. Cally Jo [Calle Johansson]. And Olie [Olaf Kolzig]. We know what we've got to do!"

The players came together and yelled the same yell they'd offered before every game of the playoffs. "Just . . . win!" They cheered and hollered and headed for the ice, where they would be greeted by the loudest hockey crowd in Washington history, most of them wearing white, all of them screaming at the top of their lungs, hoping to lift their team to victory and back into the series.

Thirty-five seconds into the game, the Red Wings scored, and all of that passion, all of that emotion, drained from the building in a heartbeat.

"The third game, they scored in 35 seconds," Wilson says. "All of our plans went right out the window. It wasn't the fact that they scored the first goal. It was the fact that their first scoring chance was always the first goal. It could be 25 or 30 seconds into the game, it could be ten minutes into the game. We make a mistake, boom, it ends up in our net. The Red Wings were feeling confident. We weren't. And we were playing catch-up hockey with a very good – no, a great, well-coached team that has been there before. It's as simple as that."

The final score was 2–1, Red Wings. Detroit held a 3–0 lead in the series. Only once before in the history of the Stanley Cup finals had a team come back from a 3–0 disadvantage to win; the Toronto Maple Leafs did it in 1942. So it could happen, like lightning could strike or you could win the lottery. But even Wilson had stopped pretending that it was a real possibility.

Just how disappointing was it, he was asked after the game, to reach the Stanley Cup finals and then find yourself one game from being swept?

No quips this time. No fables about triumphing over impossible odds.

"I don't want to answer questions," Wilson said, his voice flat, drained, defeated, "where the answer is obvious."

᠃

THE THEME OF THE Game Four sermon could be summed up simply: grasping at straws.

"I'm sure if I was up three to nothing, all I'd be thinking about is the Stanley Cup," Wilson said. "I'm sure a lot of their players are thinking the same thing. Get it over with fast. Maybe we can use that to our advantage. You get a little nervous, a little overexcited, and if we're patient, if we take advantage of some mistakes, if we're hustling, maybe we can force some extra mistakes and maybe we can turn the tide of this. . . .

"We have nothing to lose now. We've just got to go out there and try to win one game."

For the first ten minutes of the game, the Washington Capitals played as well as they had at any time during the finals, perhaps at any time during the playoffs. Then, at 10:30 of the first period, Sergei Fedorov scored for the Red Wings, and Detroit took control of the game. Martin Lapointe made it 2−0. Brian Bellows got one back for Washington in the second, but then Larry Murphy scored a power-play goal five minutes later, and that was it. The final score was 4−1. The series finished 4−0. For the fourth year in succession, the Stanley Cup had been won in a sweep.

"It came down to skill," Wilson admits. "And the Red Wings were a better hockey team than the Washington Capitals. The only regret I have is seeing how upset some guys were after we lost. They realized at that point, too late, how close they came. The look in some people's eyes – they realized they may not ever come here again. Half of my team, the young ones, believes that next June we're going to be standing there hoisting the Stanley Cup. They think that's going to happen all the time. But from my experience, from watching hockey through all these years, I know how hard it is to win the Stanley Cup."

Immediately after the game, Bowman and Wilson shook hands on the ice and exchanged a few words. "What Scotty said was, 'There's not much you could have done, Ron. Our team is that much better than yours.' I didn't take that as an insult at all. Basically, Scotty was right. . . .

"How can you be embarrassed and say that we're losers? There's 24 other teams that would have died to get swept four straight in the Stanley Cup final. I know that for a fact. I'm very proud of our team. It was a roller-coaster year but when I think back to the finals now, I understand that the outcome was inevitable. They were a much better team than we were."

While Wilson and Bowman were chatting, the Wings were celebrating their triumph A year before, Steve Yzerman had carried the Cup on a triumphant lap around Joe Louis Arena, acknowledging Detroit's first championship in more than 40 years. This time, Yzerman repeated the skate, knowing that he'd added an extra personal honour, taking home the Conn Smythe Trophy as the most valuable player in the playoffs.

But this time his picture would not be the enduring image that went with the Wings' second Stanley Cup in as many years.

Instead, it was the sight of Konstantinov, wearing his red Detroit jersey. He was wheeled to centre ice during the post-game celebrations and was at the centre of the mob as the team assembled for the traditional, goofy, smiling, laughing, celebratory photo. He was smiling along with his teammates. On his lap sat the Stanley Cup.

*Vladimir Konstantinov provided the enduring image of Detroit's 1997–98
Stanley Cup win: wheelchair-bound, holding the Cup in his lap amid a throng
of teammates.*

ACKNOWLEDGEMENTS

The Publishers are grateful to Michael Levine, who proposed this book, to White Pine Productions (notably Peter Raymont, Joseph Blasioli and Maria Pimentel) and to the CBC (notably Nancy Lee and Dan Henry) for the help given to bring this book into existence. Special thanks are due for their provision of the images from the series which appear here as photographs, selected and captioned by Doug Hunter.

ABOUT THE AUTHOR

Stephen Brunt has been a sports columnist for the *Globe and Mail* since 1988. Before that, he worked as a news reporter, covering several federal and provincial elections, and reviewed music, particularly jazz and pop.

His writing has appeared in *Esquire*, *ESPN Magazine*, *Toronto Life*, and *Report on Business*, and he is the author of several books including *Diamond Dreams*, a history of the Toronto Blue Jays.

A regular commentator on TSN and TVOntario, and a frequent contributor to CBC Radio, he also appears weekly on the nationally syndicated radio program *Prime Time Sports*.

In the course of a distinguished writing career, he has won the Michener Award, Canada's highest award for public service journalism, and the National Magazine Awards gold medal for profile writing; he has also been a three-time finalist for the National Newspaper Award, and a runner-up for the top prize of the Centre for Investigative Journalism.

Stephen Brunt lives in Hamilton, Ontario, with his wife, freelance writer Jeanie MacFarlane, and their three children.